# THE SMALL BUSINESS SURVIVAL

## 134 Troubleshooting Tips for Success

## John Ventura

Dearborn
Financial Publishing, Inc.

While a great deal of care has been taken to provide accurate and current information, the ideas, suggestions, general principles and conclusions presented in this text are subject to local, state and federal laws and regulations, court cases and any revisions of same. The reader is thus urged to consult legal counsel regarding any points of law—this publication should not be used as a substitute for competent legal advice.

Publisher: Kathleen A. Welton
Acquisitions Editor: Patrick J. Hogan
Associate Editor: Karen A. Christensen
Managing Editor: Jack L. Kiburz
Interior Design: Professional Resources & Communications, Inc.
Cover Design: Salvatore Concialdi

Published by Dearborn Financial Publishing, Inc.

Printed in the United States of America

94 95 96 10 9 8 7 6 5 4 3 2 1

**Library of Congress Cataloging-in-Publication Data**

Ventura, John.
    The small business survival kit: 134 troubleshooting tips for success / John Ventura.
         p.    cm.
    Includes bibliographical references and index.
    ISBN 0-79310-608-7 :
    1. Small business—United States—Management. 2. New business enterprises—United States—Management. 3. Success in business—United States.  I. Title.
HD62.7.V46 1994                        94-14785
658.02'2—dc20                         CIP

# Dedication

To Mary Ellen
"Grow old along with me! The best is yet to be."
—Robert Browning

# Books by John Ventura

*The Bankruptcy Kit*

*The Credit Repair Kit*

*Fresh Start!*

# Acknowledgments

When you acknowledge people, you are saying that they gave something special to you that helped in some way with the book. Reflecting on this past year, I would have to acknowledge the help of the following people:

I want to acknowledge and thank Mary Reed—my gratitude for her efforts on this book can never be fully expressed; Patrick Hogan, my editor, who kept the vision of the book clear; and Pat Wiggenhorn, whose enthusiasm for my book comes out in the way she takes my words and shapes them into something that sparkles. I also want to acknowledge Kathy Welton, publisher at Dearborn, who found me, started my writing career and has guided that career with good judgment. Thanks also to Charlie Lilly, national sales director at Dearborn, whose sales savvy gets my books in the bookstores and whose sense of humor keeps me smiling. A very special acknowledgment is needed for my mother, Lucille Ventura, who died while I was writing this book. My mother prayed for me and my success while she was alive, and I know she still prays for me.

# Contents

# Preface

*I*t is commonly acknowledged that the entrepreneur is the lifeblood of the U.S. economy. Though the economy is showing signs of real growth, major corporations continue to announce the layoffs of thousands of employees. Small business, however, accounts for 90 percent of all new private jobs, 54 percent of our country's sales and 50 percent of the gross national product (GNP)!

While making this contribution, you also take substantial risk. The failure rate of small business is very high. If you find yourself struggling, you are hardly alone. Nearly one million businesses are established every year in the United States. Of these, approximately 24 percent will fail after two years, 52 percent after four years and 63 percent after six years.

This book has been written for the smallest of the small businesses—the *Mom and Pop operations*. Such businesses generally employ fewer than 30 people and are usually sole proprietorships; although some are partnerships or corporations. These businesses are especially vulnerable to the challenges of internal and external financial difficulties. But my advice and strategies are appropriate for any small business facing financial problems.

During my 15 years of practice as a bankruptcy attorney, I have counseled many small business owners who were experiencing serious financial difficulty. Often these individuals were contemplating bankruptcy as a last-ditch effort to hold on to personal assets or save the business they had struggled to build. I have seen firsthand the emotional and financial price small business owners pay to keep a failing business afloat. In many cases, I was frustrated that I had not met many of my bankruptcy clients earlier; often the price they paid didn't have to be so high.

*The Small Business Survival Kit* contains my advice coupled with interviews with CPAs, bankers, turnaround specialists and other attorneys. Our collective proven strategies and practical ideas are offered to help you keep your business in a survival mode and—

- identify financial problems as early as possible;
- honestly appraise your chances for survival;
- effectively deal with stress and emotions as you face problems;
- quickly address problems with the IRS, the most common cause of business failure;
- assess exit strategies ahead of time, including the option of last resort, bankruptcy; and
- understand the intricacies of Chapter 7, Chapter 11 and Chapter 13 bankruptcy proceedings.

Underlying this information and advice is the philosophy that at every stage of a small business's development, you the owner(s) must pursue a defensive strategy that will help you minimize risks and maximize your chances for success.

It is the rare entrepreneur who does not experience financial difficulties. Most recent books written to help entrepreneurs start and manage their businesses assume success, not struggle and possible failure. I have attempted to offer a balance here—a dose of reality.

How often have you read in small business magazines of hugely successful entrepreneurs who failed before they hit it big? *The Small Business Survival Kit* is designed to teach you how to recognize warning signs *before* they occur, so that you can prepare for them wisely, not in the throes of panic. True success involves anticipating, preparing for and overcoming financial difficulty. I wish continued success to each of you.

# Why Small Businesses Fail

## A Day in the Office

*Even if small business owners are not contemplating bankruptcy, they often have a need for financial advice. I usually have several appointments a day with small business owners. One such day stands out in my mind.*

*Andrew W. came to see me in the morning. Taxing authorities were threatening to close down his two movie theaters because he had not paid his taxes in two years.*

*Then came Rudolf A., the owner of a small grocery store. Things had gone from bad to worse for him. Rudolph was now four months behind on a bank note, had not paid an important supplier for four months and had used money he took in from the sale of state lottery tickets to pay his own bills rather than turning the money over to the state.*

*Next came Maria C., the owner of a security business with offices in several cities. For years, Maria had paid her guards as contract labor. Now the IRS was saying that the guards had been misclassified and that Maria owed the agency thousands of dollars.*

*In the afternoon, I saw Sylvia B. who was struggling to save a small manufacturing company that she had inherited from her husband. Although the business was deeply in debt, Sylvia believed it could be saved if its debts were brought under control.*

*Allan F. came next. He owned three restaurants, all barely making money and not enough to pay the bills. Allan was trying to decide whether he should close down or sell one or more restaurant and keep the rest open or reorganize.*

---

In my practice, I usually have more individual clients than business owners. The day above was an exception, but it reminded me of how hard it is to run a successful small business in today's economy.

There are several reasons for this, including:

- lack of advance planning;
- poor business management skills;
- insufficient knowledge of the many low-cost/no-cost sources of business management advice and assistance;
- lack of attention to the day-to-day details of running a business;
- inadequate financial resources and lack of adequate cash;
- inappropriate legal structure;
- failure to keep up with obligations to the IRS and other taxing authorities;
- changes in market, economy or technology; and
- failure to face reality.

In this chapter, I will discuss many of the obstacles faced by small businesses today and provide an overview of the topics that I will be addressing in subsequent chapters.

## Planning

Good planning is fundamental when starting a new business. Planning helps you to consider all the factors critical to your success. Planning can also highlight business concepts that are simply not viable, helping you to avoid the financial and emotional struggles that come with trying to nurse a business that never should have been started in the first place.

It is not uncommon to become so enamored with a business idea that you fail to realistically assess its feasibility, adequately plan for the realities of running the business and take the time to identify the keys to business success. Many entrepreneurs pursue business concepts that are not viable or overlook important risks and stumbling blocks to success thereby failing to develop a well-thought-out plan for survival.

Up-front business planning includes:

- preparation of cash flow projections;
- preparation of pro forma income and expense statements;
- preparation of pro forma balance sheets;
- analysis of financing needs and sources;
- analysis of the skills, knowledge and technology needed for business success and the sources of same;
- finding a supportive banker;
- locating a good accountant (unless you have strong skills in this area);
- development of an adequate marketing program;
- consultation with a reputable bankruptcy attorney to discuss the best form of legal structure and learn to identify the early signs of financial trouble.

## Management Skill, Knowledge and Attention to Details

Small business owners are usually *idea people*, but business success requires more than a great idea. Success requires management skills, business knowledge and the ability to stay focused on the myriad details inherent in running a business. To be successful, a business owner must understand how to use cash flow as a management tool; know how to use and interpret financial reports; understand the signs of financial problems and how to spot them; and know how to analyze options and act decisively when problems develop.

Buoyed by enthusiasm and the entrepreneurial spirit, small business owners too often plunge into business with little or no thought about what it will take to sustain their business. Many focus on the areas of business they know the most about or are best at and ignore other aspects. A successful salesperson, for example, may open a business and focus his or her energies on generating sales. The salesperson would believe that the business was succeeding if sales volume were growing. However, unless the sales-oriented business owner expends an equal amount of energy monitoring the business's expenses and identifying ways to minimize them, he or she may actually sell themselves out of business!

It is common for small business owners to lack strong management skills or be strong in a few areas and weak in others. Furthermore, most entrepreneurs do not have the financial resources to hire employees or independent contractors with the skills and knowledge they need.

Even small business owners who understand the importance of strong management skills and recognize their own areas of weakness often do not take time to improve their skills and knowledge. Consequently, they face an uphill battle as they struggle to make their businesses work. See Figure 1.1 for some low-cost/no-cost sources of assistance.

## Financial Resources and Cash Reserves

Inadequate operating capital, especially in the early years of a business, can be a major deterrent to business success. More than two-thirds of all new small businesses start with less than $10,000 in total assets, and nearly half begin with less than $5,000—usually provided by the owners of the business, their friends and/or their family.

Limited by the conservative policies of traditional sources of start-up and operating capital, such as banks and venture capitalists, most small businesses use external financing only occasionally. When small businesses do seek external financing, their cost of borrowing is usually higher than if they were a relatively large business.

Given the inability to locate adequate capital, many small businesses struggle from the start. Even after surviving the early years, small businesses often find it difficult to grow since each new stage in their development usually requires additional capital.

Problems created by inadequate financing are complicated by the fact that many small businesses either fail to keep an adequate supply of cash reserves on hand or have no cash reserves at all.

**Figure 1.1    Low-Cost/No-Cost Sources of Assistance to Small Business Owners**

There are many ways (often free or inexpensive) to acquire the skills and the knowledge you may need to run a successful business. They include:

- Attend classes at a college or university in your area.

- Schedule a meeting with a representative of the Service Corps of Retired Executives (SCORE). These retired business owners and managers volunteer their time to provide education and guidance to small business owners in a broad range of business areas. To find the SCORE office nearest you, check the federal government listing section of your telephone directory under Small Business Administration (SBA).

- Call the graduate or undergraduate school of business in your area to see if they offer counseling to small businesses. Some schools do this in order to provide their students with real-life experiences solving business problems.

- Contact your area's Chamber of Commerce. They often sponsor seminars or run a small business assistance program.

- Find out if your state or local government has a Commerce Department or a business development/economic development office that works with small businesses. Small Business Development Centers (SBDCs) are often the single best one-stop educational and advice resource for small business.

- Ask your banker, accountant or other small business owners if they are aware of low-cost/no-cost community resources you might contact.

When a problem develops, such as a slow-paying customer, a customer check that bounces or an unexpected equipment failure, the business has no way to cover the cash shortfall. A small business, especially one without a line of credit from its bank, should have several months worth of operating expenses in the bank at all times as a cushion for such eventualities.

**Figure 1.2   Pros and Cons of Business Legal Structures**

### Sole Proprietorships

*Pros*

- Simple and straightforward to establish
- Can be established for little or no cost
- Inexpensive to run
- Can file Chapter 13 bankruptcy—inexpensive means of reorganization, see Chapter 11

*Cons*

- Tends to have a particularly difficult time getting adequate financing
- Debts and assets legally treated as the debts and assets of the sole proprietor, so business owner assumes personal liability for all business debt
- Owner legally liable for any business-related legal problems that may develop
- Ownership limited to one person

### Partnerships

*Pros*

- Multiple owners permitted
- Potential for management expertise and adequate capital greater than in a sole proprietorship
- Adequate financing easier to obtain

*Cons*

- Partners financially and legally liable for business
- Partners liable for actions of all other partners
- Can't file a Chapter 13 bankruptcy

**Figure 1.2   Pros and Cons of Business Legal Structures (Continued)**

## Corporations

### Pros

- Generally, owners have no personal financial or legal liability for business, although an increasing number of lending institutions are requiring personal guarantees of debt by owners of corporations

- Relatively easy to obtain loans and investment capital

- Can borrow money without putting owners' assets in jeopardy

- Increased tax deductions

### Cons

- Expensive and time-consuming to set up

- More complicated tax laws

- Business income taxed twice—on corporate profits and on shareholder dividends (however, Subchapter S Corporation income passes through to be taxed at shareholders' personal rate)

- If reorganizing, must file Chapter 11—a more expensive form of reorganization

## Legal Structure

Small business owners do not always consider the best legal structure for their businesses. As a result, they may not understand the pros and cons of one form of business compared to another. Figure 1.2 contains an outline of the strengths and weaknesses of the three most common types of business structures. Keep in mind that you can change the legal structure of your business as new opportunities develop or serious business problems surface.

## Tax Problems

Problems with taxes—especially with the IRS—are among the most common reasons for small business failure. Sometimes this is because business owners don't take the time to understand their tax obligations or the distinctions between employees and independent contractors. At other times, business owners ignore tax responsibilities or simply do not have the funds to meet their obligations. Chapters 5 through 7 address in detail potential problems with the IRS.

## Market, Economic and Technological Change

We live in a dynamic and rapidly changing world. Overnight, new technologies are transforming the way we do business. And as the world moves toward a global market, the economies of the world are becoming increasingly interdependent.

Succeeding in such a business environment requires all owners, no matter the size of their businesses, to keep their fingers on the pulse of their local, state, national and even international economies. Business owners must have the resources in place to upgrade or change technologies as necessary and stay attuned to the activities of the competition.

## Failure To Face Reality

It is natural to have a strong emotional attachment to a company and an overly optimistic belief in its ability to succeed. This perspective, however, can cause problems to be avoided or ignored. Such avoidance can result in a minor to moderately serious problem becoming a serious, sometimes fatal one. Dealing with problems early on increases the number of options available for handling business difficulties.

## Conclusion

Opening a business is exciting, challenging and exhausting. It is crucial that every potential business owner combines a solid business concept with good planning. Luck is also necessary if a new venture is going to succeed.

Be alert to the warning signs—where things can go wrong and what must be done if your business encounters financial difficulties. Realize the importance of immediate, decisive action. To increase the odds of your business success, the following chapters show you how to identify problems early on and engage in proactive problem solving.

# 2

# The Human Side of Crisis Management

*D*ealing with a business in financial crisis can be an emotionally draining experience for even the most self-confident business owner. Anxiety about money troubles and meeting financial obligations, along with worry about the impact that your business's problems may have on your family, can undermine your ability to logically assess your options and successfully pursue your best course of action. Additionally, the pressure of dealing with demanding creditors and insecure or worried employees can add to day-to-day stress. Unless you find relief from the unrelenting worry and pressure of serious money troubles and get adequate rest, both your ability to make sound decisions and your health can be seriously compromised.

I begin this chapter with a discussion of the importance of facing up to serious business problems as soon as possible and dealing with them realistically. Next, I provide practical suggestions for coping with the many emotions that often accompany serious business difficulty. I also include recommendations for things you can do to help your family cope with the effects of your business troubles and suggest how to deal with employees, unhappy creditors and customers.

## Acknowledging That Your Business Is in Trouble

Before you can resolve your business's problems, you must acknowledge their existence. This may sound overly simplistic, but many business owners spend valuable weeks, even months, avoiding the truth about the financial condition of their businesses. It is always difficult to face the fact that your business is in serious trouble and that painful steps may be necessary.

It is imperative that you deal with serious business troubles as soon as possible, rather than ignoring them or hoping that they will get better on their own. The longer you resist facing up to problems in your business, the more likely they will worsen and new problems will develop. Left unaddressed, the options you have for dealing with problems will diminish. Therefore, at the first sign of trouble, swallow your pride, face up to your problems, and with logic—not ego—determine the causes of your business's difficulties and what you can do about them.

### Dealing with Anger

When you begin to confront the financial condition of your business, you may begin to feel anger and start looking for scapegoats. These are common responses to serious business crises. In fact, such responses can often be very justified. Playing the blame game or dwelling on your anger, however, are not productive uses of your time or your energy. Such activity can only create more stress and cause you to lose focus on what should be uppermost in your life—establishing and implementing a plan of action for the resolution of your financial difficulties.

Sometimes anger can be justified. For example, if your bank lied to you and as a result directly contributed to your financial problems, you may have the basis for a lender liability suit and should consult a reputable attorney. But, do so only if your actions will not detract from your immediate ability to resolve your business's financial problems.

### Panic and Self-Doubt

When your life is in crisis, when you are unsure which way to turn, when you feel like you've lost control and you fear the worst, panic and self-doubt can overwhelm logic and calm. If you begin to experience paralyzing feelings, do what you can to dispel them.

Some excellent ways to overcome panic include deep-breathing exercises, restful music or a long walk. Use whatever works to shake off your panic and clear your head. Once you feel calm, take out a piece of paper, and list all possible options for dealing with your financial situation. Then, next to each option, note its pros and cons and the factors key to its success.

A sample problem:

For example, the problem could be that you're behind on paying payroll taxes. Your list of options could look like this:

1. Sell something to get the money to catch up.
2. Borrow the money if credit can be found.
3. Negotiate a payout with the IRS.
4. Close the business.
5. Use bankruptcy reorganization to pay out the IRS over five years. The pros and cons will depend on your situation and resources.

This process can help you create a simple analytical framework for logically evaluating the feasibility of your options. As you work your way through the process, you'll begin to gain a sense of control over your life, and your panicky feelings will subside.

Another good way to reduce panic is to make a list of doable short-term and long-term goals for your business, including the tasks you must accomplish to achieve each goal. (Be sure to establish reasonable deadlines.)

Sometimes, when you need to respond to serious business problems with decisiveness and confidence, you may find yourself second-guessing the wisdom of past decisions and questioning your abilities. To avoid this reaction, try to keep your business troubles in perspective by acknowledging the role you may have played in creating them without being overly hard on yourself.

---

**Survival Tip #1**

**Rather than dwelling on past mistakes, consider what you can learn from them. If your business crisis highlights a weakness, think about ways that you can address that weakness.**

---

Remember, you are not the first nor the last person to confront serious business problems. Nearly every day there is a media report about a business that is downsizing, closing its doors or filing for bankruptcy. Many of these businesses were much better financed than yours, and some even had access to the wisdom of highly paid advisors!

## The Role of Professional Advisors, Associates and Friends

When faced with difficult decisions, it can be helpful to seek advice from those you trust. By talking and brainstorming with others, you may find that you are minimizing an important consideration or overlooking a viable option. You may get emotional support as well. Persons to talk to might include your accountant or lawyer, business colleagues, friends and family members. Your accountant may be able to identify important cost cutting measures that you had overlooked. Business colleagues may be able to help you identify a new market for your product or service or a more effective way of targeting your existing markets.

Be open to new or different perspectives, but at the same time, don't allow yourself to be overly influenced by the opinions and ideas of others. Evaluate their advice and input without emotion or false hope, and maintain confidence in your own ability to select the approach that you truly believe is best. Whatever direction you decide to pursue, it is critical that you resolve your business problems in a way that you can get behind 100 percent.

## When Procrastination Is a Problem

Procrastinators can find a million excuses for avoiding something unpleasant, and procrastination is a common response to difficult problems. Procrastinating will not make a problem go away; often it makes matters worse.

Here are some things you can do to avoid procrastination:

- Write down your goals for a particular week, and then list the tasks you need to accomplish each day to achieve those goals. Categorize the tasks in order of importance. As you accomplish a task, scratch it off your list.

- Each morning when you are at your freshest, tackle the most onerous task on your list. By getting an especially difficult task out of the way first, you'll experience a sense of accomplishment and relief. You'll also find that the rest of your day will be easier knowing that you've achieved something difficult.

- When you are going to tackle a task that you have been avoiding, establish the day you will begin working on it, and stick to that schedule.

## Stress Busters

As you work your way out of trouble, don't let stress and worry derail your progress—too much of it can be debilitating. Stress and worry can cause sleep loss, lack of energy and an inability to focus at the very time that you need to be operating at maximum efficiency.

The best way to combat negative feelings is to make time in your life for pleasurable, relaxing activities, get adequate rest, exercise and eat healthy food. Here are some low-cost/no-cost activities you can pursue alone or with family or friends:

- Enjoy a picnic at your favorite park.
- Rent a video rather than going to a movie
- Go for a bike ride, or take a walk in the woods.
- Organize a potluck meal with friends.
- Practice yoga or meditation.
- Listen to music.
- Visit a museum or an art gallery.
- Register for a class at your local community college.
- Take up gardening.

---

## Survival Tip #2

**Don't rely on alcohol or drugs to relax. They can impair your decision making and jeopardize your health.**

---

Sports and volunteer activities are two other excellent ways to combat stress and bolster self-esteem. Intense physical activity is relaxing, and its benefits—weight loss, increased muscle tone, reduced lethargy, new friendships and a sense of accomplishment—can make you feel good about yourself.

## *Dawn of a New Day*

*Eric H. was the owner of a small drugstore that was being driven out of business by the discount prices of the major chains in his area. During our initial meeting, it was painfully obvious that there was little Eric could do to save his business; we discussed bankruptcy.*

*Throughout our conversation, Eric surprised me. Although he did not act cheerful, he did not display any of the usual signs of stress I'd come to expect from my clients. I was curious about the way he was dealing with his business crisis, so I asked him his secret.*

*Eric told me that he was sad about what was happening and had a few regrets, but he was already planning what he would do next. He attributed his positive attitude and lack of stress—despite his business situation—to his morning run.*

*That explanation sounded simplistic, so I asked Eric to explain. He told me that every morning he would get up before daybreak and jog through his neighborhood for 30 to 45 minutes. Eric reported that as he jogged, he would think about his problems and would usually come up with solutions for some of them. At the end of his jog, Eric felt refreshed and confident.*

*Eric also told me that his morning ritual included watching the sun come up. He could see the rising sun clearly during his jog, and the sight of it always left him somewhat awed. Eric explained that the rising sun and the special beauty of daybreak inevitably left him feeling hopeful and certain that he could handle any problem he might encounter that day.*

### Survival Tip #3

**Avoid the temptation to put off relaxation with the excuse that you're too busy. Make time. You'll deal with your problems more effectively and efficiently as a result.**

## Counseling

Sometimes, despite your best efforts, it can be impossible to shake off negative, debilitating feelings. If this happens, it may be a good idea to see a psychologist or psychiatrist to help you work through your emotions and move forward. You may also want to use a counselor as a sounding board once you begin identifying and evaluating options for dealing with your business difficulties.

---

### A Major Panic

*Robert M. came to see me about his failing computer business. His small company employed six people, four of whom concentrated on repairs and service. Although Robert was facing some difficult and lean years, it was clear, after a careful review of his situation, that he would not have to file for bankruptcy.*

*As we discussed what he needed to do to save his business, it became very obvious that Robert was his own biggest problem. Robert had started his business after working five years at another company, and he had no preparation for the responsibilities that self-employment entailed. Now, in the face of crisis, Robert was in a major panic. He spoke fast and a bit incoherently. With so many business worries in his head, most of which he had kept to himself for months, the words just spilled out in no particular order. In order to save his business, he needed to get control of his nerves.*

*Robert's wife, Dora, accompanied him to the meeting. She, too, was upset and very worried that her husband was headed for a nervous breakdown. I was sure that this problem was taking its toll on the family. However, I was certain that if Robert could begin thinking clearly about his situation and analyze his problems with some detachment, he would be able to identify and implement some reasonable solutions to his business difficulties.*

*To help Robert, I suggested that he schedule an appointment with a counselor I knew who frequently worked with businesspeople in crisis. Robert took my advice. Although it took time, I noticed that Robert slowly gained control of his emotions. As he did, Robert's business situation began to improve.*

---

## The Importance of a Sense of Humor

Seeing the humor in things can be tough when you are faced with serious business problems. However, humor can help you maintain your emotional balance and keep things in perspective.

Be sure to make time to do things that will make you laugh. Go to a funny movie, read the comics, spend time with friends who are witty and amusing. And, whenever possible, try to find ways to joke about your troubles.

## Your Family

Many business owners with troubled businesses find that their problems create a major strain on their family relationships. Often this is because the day-to-day struggles of dealing with serious business difficulties require that you spend less time with your spouse and children. Sometimes, your spouse has to assume more of the family responsibilities. These changes may cause resentment and anger. Strained relationships can also result if business troubles require your family to tighten its belt, giving up things they enjoy or have taken for granted. Concerns about money and fears for the future coupled with fatigue may create or exacerbate tensions in your marriage, and you and your spouse may begin arguing more or withdrawing from one another. Your children may become fearful and insecure and develop behavioral problems at home or in school.

The best way to minimize the likelihood of such problems is to sit down with your family and explain that you are having difficulties. Tell family members what you are doing to resolve your business problems, explain how these actions may affect their lives and let them know what they can do to help. Invite your family to ask questions, and answer them as honestly as possible.

## Survival Tip #4

**When talking with your children, do not tell them more than they can understand or need to know, and do not use words that will needlessly alarm them.**

If you are open and honest with your family, you will make it easier for them to cope with the changes they may have to make. In addition, it is more likely that your family will become your allies, ready and willing to cut household expenses, delay vacations, work at part-time jobs, etc.

### *If Your Relationship with Your Spouse Is Already in Trouble*

The previous prescription for dealing with your family assumes that you and your spouse have a good relationship. If your marriage was troubled before your business problems developed, however, those problems may cause your domestic relationship to further deteriorate. Your spouse may offer you little or no support, recriminations about changes in lifestyle may add to the already substantial pressures you are feeling and your home situation may become a battleground.

To avoid deterioration of an already bad relationship, it is best to be realistic about what you can expect from your spouse. As difficult as it may be, avoid anger and resentment if your spouse fails to respond to your business problems as you would like. Do whatever you can to prevent your relationship from deteriorating to the point of divorce. You do not need the distraction and added pressures that divorce would bring.

---

### Survival Tip #5

**Do what you can to stabilize bad or uncertain family situations, and avoid making important decisions about them until your business problems are resolved. If necessary, seek professional counseling.**

---

## Emotions as Decision-Making Criteria

When deciding what to do about your business troubles—stay in business, file for bankruptcy or shut your doors—be sure to consider how each option is likely to affect you and your family members. Here are some of the questions you should be asking yourself:

- Do I have what it takes to pursue this course of action?
- Do I really want to spend my time and energy pursuing this option?
- Is my family up to the challenge?
- Can we handle the pressure?

- What are the sacrifices we'll have to make?
- Can my family and I live with these sacrifices?
- Do I want my family to go through this?

## Maintaining Important Personal Relationships

It is easy to become cut off from close friends and business associates when coping with serious business problems. Estrangement can happen due to embarrassment about your problems and worry and preoccupation with *putting out fires*. Close friends can provide emotional support during tough times. Reach out to your friends, and take them into your confidence. Real friends will not think less of you if you are having financial problems. They will want to help in any way they can.

Although you need not share every detail, do let your friends know that you are going through tough times and are under a lot of stress. This will help explain why you may not be socializing with your friends as much as you used to and will alert them to the fact that you need their support.

## Dealing with Customers and Creditors

Calls from customers/clients and creditors can become confrontational and demanding when a business is in trouble. However, responding to such calls in an angry or defensive manner is counterproductive.

When speaking with an angry caller, remain unemotional. At the start of conversations, let callers talk without interruptions so that they "blow off steam." Interrupting or arguing is likely to make callers angrier.

Once a caller has quieted down, repeat back the gist of what you heard to show that you were listening and understand. Then, calmly explain your situation, apologize for the fact that your business problems are affecting the caller and be clear about what you can and cannot do to resolve the situation. Also, be sure to let the caller know how to help you resolve your problems and how he or she will benefit if they help.

## Survival Tip #6

**Don't let fear cause you to avoid dealing with an angry or confrontational creditor or customer. Hiding from angry creditors and customers will only make them more irate and demanding and can create additional problems.**

When dealing with angry customers and creditors, it is helpful to understand their legal rights as well as your own. For example, ask your lawyer to explain what actions a creditor can take when you can't pay your bills; find out about the legal recourse your customers have if you are unable to meet your obligations to them. Learn as much as possible about the collections process, what happens if you get sued and under what circumstances a creditor can shut your business down. Know what you can do to protect yourself from angry creditors and customers.

Having this information will add to your peace of mind and will give you greater confidence when dealing with creditors and customers.

## Dealing with Your Employees

There is no surefire way to deal with employees when faced with a business crisis. Whom you tell, what you tell, what you say and what you ask of your employees will depend on your corporate culture and your plan for resolving your financial difficulties. If your employees have a strong sense of *esprit de corps* and you have always emphasized employee participation and teamwork, you may want to be more forthcoming about your financial difficulties than if your business were very hierarchical.

## Survival Tip #7

**If it doesn't already exist, don't try to create a sense of teamwork in the middle of the stress and turmoil of a failing business. It won't work.**

If you plan to stay in business, you will probably deal with your employees differently than if you plan to shut your doors or file a Chapter 7 bankruptcy.

---

**Survival Tip #8**

**Project a calm, self-confident attitude when dealing with your employees.**

---

Whether you call a company-wide meeting to discuss your business difficulties and plans for the future or communicate this information to key managers only, your rule of thumb should be to do and say what will best help you accomplish what you have set out to do. If it will benefit your plans, be honest with your employees about the sacrifices and changes you expect, and let them know about any layoffs you may anticipate. If it won't benefit your plans, don't share the information with your employees at this time.

## Conclusion

Getting through a financial crisis, will require you to be emotionally and physically up to the challenge so that you can make logical decisions, deal effectively with angry, worried creditors and customers and take decisive action to resolve your problems as quickly as possible. It is likely that serious financial problems will affect your family and any employees you may have. They will be worried and under stress, and you will need to help them cope with the repercussions of your business problems.

# Early Signs of
# Financial Trouble

*I*t is impossible for a small business to isolate itself totally from the possibility of financial difficulty. However, a business owner can minimize the impact of internal problems and external developments by becoming familiar with early signs of financial trouble. It is important to use all available tools to monitor the health of the business, spotting problems early in their development and becoming familiar with the steps that can be taken to address those problems.

In this chapter, I will discuss the common signs of financial trouble and how to identify potential problems. The importance of monitoring and managing cash flow as a means of detecting and addressing financial problems early in their development is emphasized. In this chapter, I will also review actions you can take to avoid developing financial problems.

## The Importance of Early Action

Every business experiences financial problems—that's part of being in business. Problems can develop for several reasons, including: business mismanagement; inadequate financing; changes in competition; economic downturns; repercussions from the financial problems of an important customer or creditor; the ill health of a business owner, etc.

Successful business owners detect problems early in their development, accurately diagnose the root cause of these problems and take decisive action to resolve them. You can do this only if you are familiar with the early signs of trouble and are adept at closely monitoring the *vital signs* of your business to detect problems. When you detect problems early, you will have more options for dealing with them before they threaten your business's health.

Abe Limon, a Harlingen, Texas, bankruptcy attorney who works with small businesses, reports that many small businesses get into trouble because they pay little attention to the financial records and details of their business and therefore do not do a good job of managing finances. Limon counsels his clients and small business owners everywhere to monitor the health of their businesses as follows:

- Regularly review and interpret important financial statements, such as the profit-and-loss statement and the balance sheet.
- Maintain tight control over cash flow through the use of cash flow projections and statements.
- Understand the financial ratios applicable to your business, and know how to use them.
- Stay on top of all accounts, especially those that have the greatest impact on your bottom line.
- Regularly review your credit policy, and adapt it as necessary to respond to changing times and circumstances.
- Monitor the general health of your local, state, national or international economies, as applicable, and remain alert for changes that can affect your business.
- Be aware of developments and changes in your industry, and understand how those changes may affect you.
- Be alert for changes in the economic health of important customers or customer groups.

**Survival Tip #9**

**If you do not know how to use financial statements and ratios, talk to your accountant or banker, take a course at a local college or university, meet with a representative of the Service Corps of Retired Executives (SCORE), or contact the federal Small Business Administration (SBA) office nearest you to learn about seminars it may be offering. Your local Chamber of Commerce may also be of assistance.**

## The Importance of Cash Flow

Lack of adequate cash is a common and potentially serious problem for many small businesses. It is essential that you know how to manage cash. To do so, you will need to become familiar with the concept of cash flow. You must understand the pattern of your cash flow—where your money comes from and where it goes—and the precise timing of that ebb and flow. Additionally, you must know what you can do to ensure that you have adequate cash to fund your operations, meet your obligations and support growth and expansion. Understanding and using cash flow can help you to develop a realistic financial plan for your business, which is essential to obtaining adequate and appropriate financing.

David H. ("Andy") Bangs, an expert on small business management and the author of *The Cash Flow Control Guide* (Upstart Publishing Company, Inc., 1990), underscores the importance of cash flow to a business by explaining, "Managing for cash flow is managing for survival. Manage cash flow effectively, and your business works. Mismanage your cash flow, and you won't be able to do much more than struggle to stay afloat and sing the cash flow blues."

Effective cash flow management will help you:

- control your expenses;
- anticipate cash shortfalls and excesses;
- know when it is time to borrow funds or sell assets to meet a cash shortfall;
- know when to reduce expenses or delay paying certain expenses to deal with an anticipated cash shortfall;

- know when there is excess cash available to replace equipment, retire debt early, etc.;
- ensure that you will have adequate cash to fund growth and expansion;
- plan for and respond to changes in technology that may affect your business, i.e., desktop publishing's effect on traditional typesetting;
- meet your financial obligations; and
- borrow money on more favorable terms.

---

## Survival Tip #10

**Whenever possible, avoid using short-term debt to fund long-term assets. Always try to use the type of debt most appropriate to what you are financing.**

---

## *A Cash Flow Problem*

*Edward O. had a small insurance business that he had built up as the result of his strong skills as a salesman. He came to see me because he never seemed to have enough money to pay his bills. The first thing I asked Edward to do was to show me his projected and actual cash flow statements for the past six months. If we were going to analyze his business to determine why he was having difficulty meeting his obligations, I needed to know how much money he had coming in and how he spent it. When Edward said he did not use cash flow statements, I asked how he kept up with his money and his bills. He said that he used his checkbook. If Edward had money in his account, he would pay his bills; if he didn't, the bills would wait.*

*I was not surprised. Over the years I have learned that many small business owners do not enjoy or understand the basics of financial management and tend to manage their businesses just as Edward did.*

*I showed Edward how to use cash flow projections and how to compare them to the actual flow of cash in his business. One week later, Edward returned to my office to review cash flow statements that he had recreated for the past six months. The statements showed that Edward was generating a good amount of money, but his overhead was eating the money up. We looked at each expense item and discussed how Edward conducted his business. As we did so, Edward was able to pinpoint the expenses that he could lower or eliminate as well as things he could do to accelerate the flow of cash into his business.*

*Once Edward took the time to generate financial reports for his business and to analyze those reports, he quickly identified problem areas, diagnosed their cause and got his business back on course with little or no damage. Edward continued to prepare cash flow projections and compare them to his actual cash flow in order to better manage his business. As a result, Edward was able to keep his finger on the pulse of his business.*

## What Is Cash Flow?

Cash flow is the difference between your cash receipts and your cash disbursements. Andy Bangs describes cash flow as "the life-blood of your business." The management of cash flow is the single most important way to ensure business success. See Figure 3.1 for clarification of common misconceptions about cash flow.

To understand and manage your cash flow, you must be familiar with your business's expenses and sources of cash. If you extend credit to your customers, you'll also need to understand your collection cycles. And, you'll need to be familiar with the timing of your cash flow—when do you make cash disbursements, and when do you receive cash income from sales, investments, refunds, etc.?

Cash may flow into your business as a result of:

- cash from operations;
- new capital investment;
- new debt;
- sale of fixed assets;
- windfall (proceeds of lawsuits);
- cash sales;
- collections on accounts receivables;
- use of a line of credit; and
- interest, royalties and refunds.

**Figure 3.1 Misconceptions about Cash Flow**

Many small business owners are unfamiliar with the concept of cash flow and how cash flow can be managed to increase business stability, profitability and growth. Here are some common misconceptions about cash flow:

- **Having a lot of cash means that your business is doing well.**

    Fact: *There can be a lot of cash flowing through your business, but if it is not timed so that adequate money is available to pay expenses, salaries, etc. as they come due, your business's financial health may suffer. Or, your cash flow may be positive because you are not paying your bills.*

- **Not having a lot of cash means your business is in trouble.**

    Fact: *If you keep your expenses to a minimum and gain the maximum benefit from your assets, and if you carefully manage your business's cash flow, you increase the likelihood of your business being healthy.*

- **If your business experiences strong sales or if its sales are increasing, it is in good financial health.**

    Fact: *If your sales are increasing but your product or service is underpriced, you may actually be losing money since revenues from your sales may not cover the cost of generating your goods or services.*

Also, if your company extends credit to its customers without adequately evaluating the effect of credit on cash flow, your financial health may be damaged despite strong sales. This is because the flow of cash into your business is not timed so that there is always sufficient money available to pay bills, salaries, taxes, etc. as they come due.

Cash may flow out of your business as a result of:

- the purchase of raw materials or inventory;
- the purchase of services and supplies;
- loan payments;
- salaries and employee benefits;
- accounts payable;
- rent or mortgage payments;
- taxes, permits;
- employee illness;
- mistakes;
- theft;
- utilities (fluctuating due to extreme weather conditions);
- price adjustments due to competition;
- slow receivables.

If you understand where your money comes from and goes to and the timing of that flow, you can better manage the process. And, through effective cash flow management, your business will be more apt to have adequate cash to meet its obligations and to make effective use of its excess cash.

## Using Cash Flow as a Management Tool

You can improve the management of cash resources by regularly projecting your cash flow and comparing those projections to actual cash flow. Doing so will help you detect financial problems as soon as they develop so that you can make necessary adjustments quickly.

Talk to your accountant or banker about how frequently you should project your cash flow. Then, use the form in Figure 3.2 to project your cash flow and compare it to actual dollars. At a minimum, your projections and comparisons should be done on a monthly or quarterly basis depending on the nature of your business. However, if your business is having financial difficulties, consider projecting cash flow on a weekly basis.

**Figure 3.2    Sample Cash Flow Form**

---

Use the cash flow form below as a model for estimating your cash flow each month and comparing your projections to your actual cash flow. Modify the form as necessary to make it applicable to your business. You can show all the months in a year on a single form, or you can use one form for each month.

## Month and Year:

|  | Estimate | Actual |
|---|---|---|
| **1. Cash on Hand:** (Start of Month) | $ _____ | _____ |
| **2. Cash Receipts** | | |
| Cash Sales | _____ | _____ |
| Collections on Accounts Receivables | _____ | _____ |
| Other Sources of Cash (Specify) | _____ | _____ |
| **3. Total Cash Receipts:** | $ _____ | _____ |
| **4. Total Cash Available:** (#1 plus #3) | $ _____ | _____ |
| **5. Cash Disbursements** | | |
| Purchases (Merchandise) | _____ | _____ |
| Gross Salaries | _____ | _____ |
| Payroll Expenses, e.g., Taxes | _____ | _____ |
| Commissions | _____ | _____ |
| Outside Services | _____ | _____ |
| Office and Operating Supplies | _____ | _____ |
| Repairs and Maintenance | _____ | _____ |
| Advertising | _____ | _____ |
| Accounting and Legal | _____ | _____ |
| Travel and Entertainment | _____ | _____ |
| Insurance | _____ | _____ |

**Figure 3.2    Sample Cash Flow Form (Continued)**

Rent or Mortgage      _____      _____
Telephone      _____      _____
Utilities      _____      _____
Taxes      _____      _____
Interest      _____      _____
Loan Payments      _____      _____
Owner's Withdrawal      _____      _____
Other Expenses (Specify)      _____      _____

*6. Total Cash Disbursements:*      $ _____      _____

*7. Net Cash Flow:*      $ _____      _____
    (#4 minus #6)

**Survival Tip #11**

**There are good software programs available to help businesses project and manage their cash flow. Check *Home Office Computing* magazine for reviews of software helpful to small businesses.**

To use the cash flow form in Figure 3.2, follow these directions:

1.  Register the amount of cash you have on hand at the start of the month.

2.  Establish realistic sales projections for the period covered by your cash flow projection. Be sure to distinguish between cash sales and credit sales. A credit sale does not generate cash; it creates a receivable. Your projections should reflect cash receipts only. (Andy Bangs suggests using a "most likely" figure for your projections. This figure represents the midway point between the cash receipts flowing into your business if every aspect of your business were to go exactly

as you wish and the cash receipts that would be generated if everything went wrong.)

3. Project other sources of anticipated cash receipts. These other sources could include payments on accounts receivables, interest income or income from an investment, income from the sale of an asset, etc.

4. Total up all cash receipts.

5. Total all cash available.

6. Project your fixed expenses—those that do not vary with your sales and anticipated variable expenses—and your variable expenses—those that change with the rise and fall of your sales. Figure 3.3 shows examples of fixed and variable expenses. An expense should be recognized when it is paid, e.g., when you actually spend cash. In other words, if you charge your office supplies, you should record the amount of cash you pay on those supplies at the point they are paid, not the amount you charged. Again, in projecting cash disbursements, it is a good idea to use the same "most likely" figure Bangs suggests.

---

### Survival Tip #12

**Talk with your accountant to be sure you don't overlook any expenses.**

---

7. Total all your cash disbursements and subtract that total from your total cash receipts. The difference is your projected net cash flow. (Item 7 on the sample form in Figure 3.2.) If the dollar figure is positive, you are projecting a positive cash flow—more cash receipts than cash disbursements. If the dollar figure is negative—more cash disbursements than cash receipts—you're projecting a negative cash flow. In other words, your projections indicate that your business will not have enough cash to meet its obligations and cover other anticipated expenses.

**Figure 3.3   Examples of Fixed and Variable Expenses**

To assist you in categorizing your expenses, following is a partial list of typical fixed and variable expenses. If you are uncertain about one of your business's expenses, talk to your accountant, the SBA or a SCORE volunteer.

| *Fixed Expenses* | *Variable Expenses* |
|---|---|
| Rent or mortgage payment | Supplies |
| Salaries | Commissions |
| Payroll taxes | Travel and entertainment |
| Loan payments | Sales Tax |
| Insurance | Utilities |
| Maintenance and cleaning | |

8. If your projected cash flow is negative, consider actions you can take to create a positive cash flow for your business. (See page 34 for a review of possible actions.) After deciding on all necessary changes, revise your projections.

9. As actual numbers come in for each period, record them on your cash flow form, and compare them to your projections. If they differ, identify the reason for the difference and any adjustments or changes you need to make to help ensure that your actual cash flow ends up positive. You also may need to review the assumptions you made in developing your projections to make sure they're valid.

## Survival Tip #13

**After you've prepared six months to a year's worth of cash flow statements—projections and actuals—review them to identify any trends, relationships, etc. that may help you do a better job of managing your business.**

## Negative Cash Flow

If your projected or actual cash flow is negative, it is important that you analyze why and identify actions you can take to improve your cash flow. If you need help figuring out why your business's cash flow is negative, consult with a financial professional, such as your accountant, banker, a representative of the SBA or a SCORE volunteer. Figure 3.4 outlines a few common causes of cash flow problems.

---

## Survival Tip #14

**Remember, if you do a lot of business on credit, increasing sales may not help an immediate cash flow problem since you will probably not receive cash from these sales for at least 30 days.**

---

Here are some actions to consider when your projected or actual cash flow is negative:

- Carefully evaluate all expenses for possible reductions or cuts. As applicable, negotiate better deals on raw materials and supplies, and negotiate the rescheduling of some of your payments.
- When appropriate, get money up front from your customers.
- Reevaluate your credit policy, or do a better job of collecting on your accounts receivables.
- Increase efforts to collect on your accounts receivables.
- Reevaluate your pricing.
- Delay paying certain creditors.
- Increase cash receipts by offering customers a discount for prompt payment on their accounts or for paying cash rather than charging.
- Liquidate unnecessary assets to generate additional cash.
- Talk to your banker about a line of credit.
- Borrow against your receivables.

**Figure 3.4   Why Cash Flow Problems Develop**

Cash flow problems can develop for many reasons. Among the most common are:

- Your fixed costs have increased without an equal increase in the amount of cash coming into your business.

- Your variable costs have increased.

- Your sales are not generating cash fast enough.

- You have too much cash tied up in inventory, supplies, etc.

## Survival Tip #15

**When deciding what to do about a negative cash flow, it is important not to do anything that will hurt the integrity of your product or service, thereby damaging your company's reputation, hurting employee morale, etc.**

### Positive Cash Flow

If your cash flow—projected or actual—is positive, it is important that you understand the reason for the excess cash. Excess cash is not necessarily a sign of good management or a great business idea. For example, your cash flow may be positive because you've overlooked an important cash obligation.

If your analysis indicates that your excess is the result of good cash management and a thriving business, then it is time to consider what to do with those funds so that they can be put to good use for your business. Here are some things to consider:

- Retire debt.
- Expand your operations.
- Hire additional personnel.
- Replace old or outdated equipment, or buy new equipment.
- Consult with your accountant about the best uses of your excess cash.

## Signs of Trouble

Regularly monitoring your cash flow and consistently using other business management tools can help you detect problems in their earliest stages. These problems often appear relatively minor. However, if left unaddressed, a minor problem can evolve into a serious, if not fatal problem. This is especially true for small businesses where there is often little room for error. Never ignore or underestimate a problem.

Although the early signs of business trouble vary depending upon the type of business, the most common signs include:

- trouble making estimated tax payments and coming up with your share of employee payroll tax dollars;
- use of employee trust fund dollars for operating capital;
- difficulty paying your bills, making loan payments, meeting payroll, etc.;
- renewing rather than paying off bank loans;
- late notices, calls and letters from your creditors and suppliers about your past due accounts;
- creditors and suppliers tightening their credit policies; or
- delaying or downsizing payment of your regular salary.

---

### Survival Tip #16

**Familiarize yourself with the federal Fair Debt Collection Practices Act (FDCPA) and any similar state laws. By doing this, you will learn what creditors and debt collectors are allowed to do to collect their money and what recourse you have if they violate FDCPA. For information about these laws, call the Federal Trade Commission (FTC) at (202) 326-2222.**

---

If your business is experiencing trouble and you fail to act, it is likely that the situation will worsen and additional problems will develop. You may find that:

- your sales begin declining because there is insufficient cash to fund them.

- your creditors and suppliers do business with you on a cash-only basis.
- your accounts are turned over to collection agencies, or your creditors and suppliers threaten you with legal action.
- you receive threatening notices from the IRS.
- your creditors demand additional collateral or threaten to call your notes.
- your bank refuses to renew your loan.
- employee turnover increases due to the growing instability of your business.
- you are unable to meet your tax obligations.

---

## Survival Tip #17

**Sol Stein, author of *A Feast for Lawyers* (M. Evans and Company, 1989), a book based on his own experience with Chapter 11 bankruptcy, recommends that at a very early stage in its operations, a small business uses more than one bank so that a single bank does not control the business.**

---

Unless you take decisive and effective action to address your problems, they will worsen and your business's financial situation will continue to deteriorate. Additionally, options for dealing with your problems will decrease. As time goes on, the options that remain will become increasingly expensive and severe, and at some point, your only option will be to file for bankruptcy.

Ignoring your business problems can lead to the following:

- The IRS seizes your assets, levies your bank accounts and pursues other enforced collection actions.
- Your creditors foreclose on and repossess your property.
- Creditors, suppliers and customers sue your business.
- You don't have enough cash to purchase the supplies, raw materials, etc. that you need to keep your business going.
- You receive an eviction notice from your landlord.
- You can't make payroll.
- Creditors threaten to put you into involuntary bankruptcy.

## Involuntary Bankruptcy

If your efforts to turn your business around are unsuccessful or if you ignore your business's growing problems, it is possible that you may be threatened with involuntary Chapter 7 bankruptcy. Creditors can take this step if they are extremely anxious about the financial health and long-term prognosis of your business and want to do what they can to protect their investment.

---

### Survival Tip #18

**Involuntary bankruptcies are very rare for small businesses since the action is an expensive one for creditors. An involuntary bankruptcy is most apt to happen when there is a lot of money at stake.**

---

If you have 12 or more creditors, any 3 of them can join together to petition the court to force you into bankruptcy when their unsecured claims amount to at least $5,000. If you have fewer than 12 creditors, a single creditor owed at least $5,000 can force you into bankruptcy.

If your creditors force you into Chapter 7, your assets will be liquidated and the proceeds distributed among your creditors just as if you had filed bankruptcy yourself. If you have signed any personal guarantees to obtain credit, your creditors will also come after your personal assets after your involuntary bankruptcy has been filed.

---

### Survival Tip #19

**Involuntary bankruptcy is most common when a business has a substantial number of unsecured assets that can be liquidated to pay its unsecured creditors.**

---

## Conclusion

In this chapter, I have emphasized the importance of understanding the signs of financial trouble and of knowing how to use all available tools for identifying problems as early as possible.

**Figure 3.5   Steps To Take To Avoid Developing Financial Problems**

There are many steps that you can take to improve management of your business and increase the likelihood that relatively minor problems do not become serious or fatal. These steps include:

1. Understand how to read and interpret key financial statements and reports, including balance sheets, income or profit and loss statements (P&Ls) and cash flow statements.

2. Stay apprised of economic changes and developments that can affect your business, its suppliers and customers by reading business publications and joining business-related clubs and organizations.

3. Network with others in your industry by joining associations that serve your industry and subscribing to industry-related newsletters and publications.

4. Upgrade and augment your management skills by attending seminars and workshops sponsored by the SBA, local colleges and universities, associations and companies that are in the business of planning and conducting seminars.

5. Minimize your dependence on a single customer or group of customers.

6. Develop and implement a cost-effective marketing plan.

7. Hire a competent accountant, or utilize the services of an accountant on a contract basis.

8. Do not take on too much debt.

9. Develop a well-thought-out plan for growth and expansion.

10. Carry adequate insurance.

11. Establish a wise credit policy.

12. Respecting the adage "an ounce of prevention is worth a pound of cure," meet with a CPA or bankruptcy attorney to discuss the steps you should take to prepare yourself for the possibility of bankruptcy and to optimize your situation if bankruptcy becomes necessary.

Detecting problems, diagnosing their causes and taking decisive action to resolve those problems are key to business success and survival. Figure 3.5 summarizes important steps to take to avoid financial problems.

# Action Steps for Survival

*A*s I emphasized in Chapter 3, business success requires small business owners to monitor the health of their businesses constantly for signs of problems and to be prepared to take decisive action at the earliest sign of trouble. This chapter provides a framework for diagnosing and dealing with the problems small business owners may uncover with an emphasis on the actions business owners can take themselves. Although use of a turn-around specialist is beyond the financial reach of most small businesses, in this chapter I will discuss the services these professionals can provide and the advantages of working with one.

## The Problem-Solving Process

The following four steps represent a logical process for addressing the immediate effects of problems and diagnosing their root cause:

1. Identify the problem.
2. Diagnose the problem.
3. Do what you can right away to address the immediate effects of the problem.

4. Develop a strategy for resolving the problem and ensuring that the problem does not recur.

If you constantly monitor your business for the earliest signs of trouble, you will probably have time to work sequentially through each step of the problem-solving process when signs appear. If your problems are not caught early enough or you do not deal with them when they appear, your business may be in crisis by the time you begin to address your dilemma. In that case, you will probably have to accomplish some of the steps in the problem-solving process concurrently, which can only add to the pressure you will inevitably be feeling.

## Involving Others in the Problem-Solving Process

When dealing with a problem, it is often helpful to involve others. For example, key employees and managers may have information and insights that can be invaluable to problem solving. One vehicle for involvement of employees and managers is the establishment of an *ad hoc* task force or committee charged with analyzing the problems of your business and identifying potential solutions. Or, you may simply want to consult informally with key staff.

Outsiders not directly involved in the day-to-day operations of your business who don't have a vested interest in it can be another useful source of insight and advice. These resources are often able to assess your situation in a more objective manner than you can. However, make sure that you consult with people who have the credentials and the expertise to provide you with good advice. Bad advice is worse than no advice at all.

### Survival Tip #20

**Don't overlook low-cost/no-cost sources of outside assistance in your community. These include the Service Corps of Retired Executives (SCORE) Program, the Small Business Administration (SBA), graduate business programs at local colleges and universities, your Chamber of Commerce and local or state business development offices. And, don't overlook your accountant, although that professional's advice will probably not be low-cost.**

**Figure 4.1   Roadblocks to Constructive Problem Solving**

---

Diagnosing your problems and identifying workable solutions requires clear thinking and analysis. The following barriers can get in the way of rational problem solving:

- Inaccurate assumptions

- Misperceptions

- Fear and other emotions

- Procrastination

- Rash actions

- Lack of detachment

- Resistance to change or an unwillingness to face reality

---

## Meet with Your Accountant and Bankruptcy Attorney

When financial problems develop, even if you feel that you understand the reasons for your problems, it is always advisable to meet with your accountant. This professional will either concur with your diagnosis and plan of action or suggest alternative causes of your problems and suggest alternative solutions.

Additionally, consult with a reputable attorney who has experience dealing with your type of business. Meeting with an attorney at this point is not an admission of failure but simply an intelligent, rational response to your situation. Your meeting should have several purposes.

First, an attorney can help you avoid spending time, energy and money chasing after a hopeless goal if your best response to your problems is to shut your business down or file for bankruptcy. If the attorney you meet with makes such a recommendation and you are not sure about following this advice, get a second opinion. If the second attorney concurs, it is probably time to prepare for the inevitable, and you should read Chapters 8 through 12.

Second, an attorney can provide you with advice and information that may help you avoid bankruptcy. And third, an attorney can identify guideposts or milestones that you can use to assess your progress in solving your problems. These guideposts will help you determine whether bankruptcy or closing your business down is your best move.

## Talk with Employees

If your business problems are serious, it is likely that your employees are aware of them, and morale may be deteriorating. This is especially true if layoffs or reductions in benefits or salaries have begun. To avoid mass resignations or a further deterioration of morale at the very time that you most need your employees' support, let your employees know as much as you feel comfortable telling them about your situation and what you are doing about it.

Do what you can to boost employee morale. Play on your employees' sense of teamwork and *esprit de corps*. Whenever appropriate, ask your employees to share ideas about things they can do to reduce expenses and increase cash flow, or establish a program that awards employees for ideas that actually save your business money.

## Sources of Assistance

It can sometimes be helpful to seek the assistance of outside experts to understand the reason(s) for payroll tax problems and what you can do about them. There are a number of sources for community-based low-cost/no-cost assistance. For example, volunteers in the Service Corps of Retired Executives (SCORE) program offer businesses one-on-one counseling and training on a wide range of business subjects. Look for SCORE under Small Business Administration (SBA) in the section of your phone book that lists federal government offices, or call the SBA office nearest you.

Other possible sources of assistance in your community may include: SBA's Small Business Development Centers and the university-based Small Business Institutes, as well as the business schools of any colleges or universities in your area. Also, your local or state government or local Chamber of Commerce may have an office of business development/assistance that could help you.

## Survival Tip #21

**If there is no listing for an SBA office in your local phone book, call (800) U ASK SBA to find out about the office closest to you.**

## Time for Soul Searching

If your operational problems are having a serious effect on your business, it is important for you to do some soul searching as you work your way through the early stages of the problem-solving process. This will help you to open yourself to the possibility that your best response to your business situation may be to cut your losses by closing your doors or filing bankruptcy. This is not the time for false hope, delusions, self-deception or the avoidance of reality. To help you in your soul searching, ask yourself the following questions:

- Are the IRS and other creditors threatening legal action? (*If yes, get the advice of a bankruptcy attorney immediately.*)

- What will it take to resolve my business problems? Do I have the resources—money, time, personnel and emotional resilience—to resolve these problems and maintain the stability of my business? If not, can I acquire these strengths? Refer back to Chapter 2 for an in-depth discussion of the role of emotion in a business crisis.

- After I trim all the fat from my business and generate as much additional cash flow as possible, will my business be able to meet its operational expenses? If not, it may be time for a liquidation bankruptcy.

- Am I personally liable for my business debts, and am I in danger of losing assets due to my business problems? (*If your answer is yes, you may need to consider filing a reorganization bankruptcy.*)

- Should I be in business at all? Do I really have the temperament, skills and background to be a successful business owner and manager? Are there changes I could easily make to accommodate my shortcomings?

- Under what conditions can my business be marketable and competitive? How much control can I have or do I have over those conditions right now, and what will it take to get greater control?
- Do I want to stay in business?

## Consider Your Legal Structure

Chapter 1 covered the pros and cons of the various types of legal structures available to small businesses and noted that a business can change its legal structure if financial problems develop and a different structure would be advantageous to the struggling business. If you are considering bankruptcy, you should give serious attention to your current legal structure because it will have great bearing on your strategy. Changing the legal structure of your business can help keep your personal assets out of the reach of creditors and the IRS and can better position you for bankruptcy. However, before changing your legal structure, it is important to weigh carefully the pros and cons of a possible change so that you do what is most appropriate.

### Sole Proprietorships

Most small businesses are set up as sole proprietorships—legal structures that make no distinction between the assets and liabilities of the business and its owner. The debts of a sole proprietorship are legally viewed as the owner's. If you are a sole proprietor, this means that you have no legal protection against the negative financial repercussions of your business's financial problems and that if you owe money to creditors, suppliers, your bank or the IRS, they can come after your personal assets—home, car, furniture, etc.—to collect their money.

There is, however, an important advantage to retaining a sole proprietorship business structure if you catch your financial problems early in their development, want to remain in business, and if your personal assets are not yet at risk. The advantage is that unless its debt is excessive, a sole proprietorship is eligible to file Chapter 13 reorganization, a relatively inexpensive and quick form of reorganization bankruptcy.

If your financial condition is deteriorating and you fear that your assets may become "at risk," you may want to consider converting from a sole proprietorship to a corporation. There are several potential advantages to such a conversion. For example, if you convert to a corporation, you may be able to keep your business running long enough to pay off all or a large percentage of the liabilities you acquired as a sole proprietor. Then, when you file for bankruptcy, your personal assets will not be exposed. However, if you anticipate needing to do additional borrowing in order to keep your business running after you've incorporated, you may still be required to personally guarantee any new credit you obtain.

## Survival Tip #22

**You may be eligible for a Subchapter S corporation status that would allow you to avoid some of the drawbacks of a regular corporation. Talk with an attorney about this.**

If you are considering converting from a sole proprietorship to a corporation, do so only if you are absolutely certain that you will not have to assume personal liability for future debt. And remember, if your financial situation is shaky, if you do not already have an excellent relationship with your bank and other creditors or if you lack adequate collateral, you probably will have to pledge a personal guarantee even if you're incorporated.

There are other drawbacks to converting from a sole proprietorship to a corporation. It takes a significant amount of expense, paperwork and time to incorporate and to operate as a corporation. You will have to file the appropriate paperwork with your state, and most states will charge you an initial filing fee as well as an annual fee. You will need to write bylaws that spell out how your corporation will be run, and you'll have to comply with all your state's formal requirements for doing business as a corporation. You'll also need to maintain a bank account and business records totally separate from your personal accounts and records, and you'll be required to file corporate income tax returns and to pay taxes on all profits that your corporation may earn.

If you want to reorganize, the second drawback is that a corporation must file a Chapter 11 reorganization bankruptcy rather than a Chapter 13. And the vast majority of Chapter 11s, especially among small businesses, eventually end up being converted into Chapter 7 liquidations.

---

### Survival Tip #23

**Before converting a corporation to a sole proprietorship, be sure that your debt does not disqualify you for Chapter 13. To be eligible you cannot owe more than $100,000 in unsecured debt or more than $350,000 in secured debt.**

---

## Corporations

If your business is incorporated, you have shielded yourself from personal liability for your business problems except in those instances where you have given a creditor a personal guarantee. Therefore, don't do anything that might jeopardize that protection, such as not paying your corporate franchise taxes or your payroll taxes, writing hot checks or dealing with suppliers in a manner that leads them to believe that you are assuming personal liability.

If you are contemplating a reorganization bankruptcy and your liabilities are relatively limited, e.g., do not exceed the maximums for filing a Chapter 13 reorganization, it is a good idea—if possible—to convert your business's legal structure to a sole proprietorship and then to file bankruptcy immediately. This move assumes that you are the sole shareholder in your corporation. If you are not, you will have to buy out all other shareholders, something that might not be financially feasible.

## Partnerships

Members of a partnership are personally and equally liable for the obligations of the business, just as a sole proprietor is. This means that if your partner borrows additional money or does something outside normal business practices in an effort to cope with the problems of the business, you are personally liable for these actions even if you were unaware of what was being done or told your partner not to do it. Therefore, if you are in a financially troubled partnership and you are not interested in reorganizing, it may be advisable to get out of the partnership.

**Survival Tip #24**

**If you are in a limited liability partnership, you have less potential exposure than in a general partnership. However, members of a limited liability partnership are equally liable for payroll taxes.**

There are several ways to exit a partnership. If you intend to remain in business, you may want to consider buying out your partner and assuming full control of the business. Then if you want to reorganize, you can use Chapter 13, assuming your debt does not exceed the allowable maximums.

Another way to exit a partnership is to have your partner buy you out. However, even after you are bought out, you will continue to be liable for all obligations incurred by the partnership prior to the buy out, and you will no longer have any say in the way the business is run. This could leave you in a very vulnerable position if your former partner allows the business to deteriorate.

Your third option is to dissolve your partnership. When considering whether or not to remain in a partnership, be sure to weigh the benefits and the disadvantages of the business structure. For example, the benefits of partnership include such things as added management expertise and easier access to capital, as well as avoidance of the double taxation whammy that corporations other than Subchapter S businesses get hit with. These advantages may outweigh the risks related to remaining in a partnership. On the other hand, if you remain in a partnership and bankruptcy becomes a necessity, be forewarned that the only type of reorganization bankruptcy you will be able to file is Chapter 11, an expensive and time-consuming option.

## Diagnosing the Problem

Accurate diagnosis of the severity and cause of your business problems is essential to resolving and preventing their recurrence. Adam Radzick, a New Jersey-based professional who helps financially troubled businesses "get back on their feet," uses a medical analogy to highlight the importance of a good diagnosis. "If a medical doctor thinks that his patient has a cold and he is plying the patient with aspirin and cold compresses when the patient actually has a kidney problem, the doctor can prescribe as many compresses and aspirin as he wants and they are not going to help. However, with the correct diagnosis, the solution becomes apparent."

Exactly how you should go about diagnosing your business problems will depend on the nature of your business and the symptoms that you are experiencing. You will probably need to review financial records, reports and other data to identify trends and changes and to evaluate the efficiency and effectiveness of your business operations. You may also need to assess trends and changes in the general economy—as well as in your industry and among your customers—and you may need to talk with managers or other key employees in your business.

Avoid being too willing to blame outside factors for your business problems. According to Radzick, you can almost always find companies similar to yours, dealing with the very same external pressures, who are doing fine. In most cases, the real cause of business troubles is internal.

Although every small business is unique, here are some common causes of financial difficulty:

- Expenses that exceed revenues
- Improper or inadequate financing
- Overly rapid growth funded by debt rather than by business profit
- Overly rapid growth that outpaces a business's operating systems, the skills and abilities of its personnel, etc.
- Inadequate management controls
- Poor management skills and business know-how among business owners/key management
- Ineffective mechanisms for decision-making and problem-solving
- Inadequate attention to marketing or an ineffective marketing program
- Failure to stay competitive by keeping up with changing technologies
- Failure to maximize a business's competitive strengths and to capitalize on its competitors' weaknesses
- Overreliance on a single customer or a single customer group
- Key customer groups experiencing a financial downturn
- A poor or faulty product or service

- A product or service that is insufficiently differentiated from the competition's
- Lack of an adequate market for a product or service
- Employee problems—poor productivity, inadequate skills or knowledge, low morale, etc.
- Unwillingness to look objectively at business difficulties
- General economic downturn

---

## Survival Tip #25

**The more quickly you assess the financial health of your business, the more options you will have for dealing with the problems.**

---

## Planning a Course of Action

Once you have accurately diagnosed the fundamental causes of your business problems and assessed your business's overall health, it's time to decide what to do. If your business is still viable, it is time to develop a *game plan* for constructive action.

Your game plan should lay out a course of action for alleviating the negative impact of your business problems on operations and for restoring your business to health. The plan should also identify all the steps necessary to prevent a recurrence of the problems.

Your plan should be realistic and attainable. It should include achievable sales goals for the next 3, 6 and 12 months, a practical strategy for meeting those goals, a profit plan based on your projections, together with doable cost-cutting measures and a realistic plan for increasing cash flow. Avoid overoptimism when developing sales projections and collections on accounts receivables. If you are overly optimistic about what you can achieve, you may fail to make necessary decisions. As a result, expect your problems to worsen rather than improve.

Most likely, your plan will involve a combination of management and operational changes to improve efficiency and increase cash flow. If your business's problems are still relatively minor, your "game plan" may require only minor tinkering as well as a tightening of both management and operations. If your business problems are more serious, your game plan may need to include negotiations with your creditors, bankers and suppliers, a total overhaul of certain areas of your business, the development of new markets, a redefinition of your product or service, etc. Most likely, recovery and ongoing business stability will also require an injection of additional capital.

Always base your plan of action on a careful analysis of your business's financial records, reports and projections as well as on current and projected market trends and the changing competition. Also, it is always a good idea to perform cost benefit analyses of each possible action to help ensure that the action will have the financial impact you desire.

Pay careful attention to the amount of money you will need to implement your game plan, and evaluate possible sources of all necessary funds. You may find that the first plan you develop is financially risky. If so, you'll need to modify your plan.

---

### Survival Tip #26

**If time allows, consider developing several possible game plans. Compare the plans on the basis of their short-term and long-term effect on your business as well as on the resources each will require and how swiftly each option can be implemented.**

---

When planning a course of action, be mindful of its probable impact on your creditors, suppliers, bankers, customers and employees. Some potential impacts will be obvious; others, however, will be more subtle. For example, certain actions could have the effect of discouraging customers from doing business with you or could make it more expensive for you to do business. When necessary, your plan of action should identify things you can do to reassure these key groups.

## Actions To Consider

The specific actions you take to stabilize your business and resolve its problems will depend on your diagnosis. Following are some possible actions to consider:

- Evaluate all expenses including business-related travel or entertainment, subscriptions, the purchase of supplies, raw materials or equipment, insurance, the use of outside professionals, postage, phone services, etc. to determine which can be reduced, delayed or eliminated.

- Eliminate or discontinue products or services that are not making money.
- Evaluate the effectiveness of your marketing activities and modify as needed.
- Assess current staffing levels to determine if there are positions that could be eliminated or consolidated without damage to your company's effectiveness and efficiency.
- Reduce staff salaries and/or benefits.
- Reduce your own salary.
- Cut prices. This action alone can sometimes provide the cash a business needs to turn itself around.
- Defer maintenance activities as long as possible.
- Increase efforts to collect your accounts receivables. Call those who owe you money, and press them for it. When necessary, use the services of a collection agency.
- Tighten your collection procedures.
- Delay paying your accounts payable as long as possible but without incurring additional charges or jeopardizing your standing with suppliers, creditors, your bank, etc.
- Increase the productivity of your sales staff through special incentives, bonuses, training, etc.
- Sell assets that are not needed, including equipment and office furniture.
- Offer incentives to employees who can identify cost-cutting measures. Often those who are on the front line are aware of waste or have creative ideas for streamlining operations.
- Expand your customer base so that you are not overly dependent on a single customer or group of customers.
- Consider moving to less expensive space or reducing the amount of space you are renting.
- Identify new sources of cash.
- Meet with your creditors, bankers and suppliers about lowering your monthly payments, restructuring debt, obtaining additional credit, etc.
- Talk to the IRS about working out a payment plan for any

back taxes. (For more information about dealing with the IRS, read Chapters 5 through 7.)

- Improve your managerial skills and business know-how by taking classes or attending seminars.

---

**Survival Tip #27**

**Consider placing a freeze on the purchase of office supplies for a specified period of time. You may be surprised by the number of supplies employees pull out of their desks, cabinets or bring from home that can help you get through this period!**

---

## Tightening Collection Policies

If your analysis of your business's financial situation points to the need to improve your cash flow by speeding up collection on your accounts receivables, you should consult with your accountant about the best way to do this. Consider the following options.

- Establish a better credit policy so that you make good decisions about extending credit; consider the use of credit cards.
- Tailor your credit policies to different customer groups based on their ability to pay or payment history.
- Develop a more effective way of monitoring your accounts receivables—speeding up *slow pays* and getting payment on delinquent accounts. Ways to accomplish these goals include: hiring additional personnel to make calls to slow pays or giving existing employees this responsibility; hiring a credit manager if, by its nature, your business must do a lot of business on credit; purchasing computer software that will facilitate the management of your receivables; and using the services of a collection agency.
- Develop a written policy for how your business will deal with slow-paying customers.
- Use a credit bureau to help you screen credit applicants.
- Require up-front money from those who had formerly had credit extended to them.

- Evaluate your terms of credit—the interest rate and penalties you charge and when these charges will start; the type of discount you offer for early payment, etc.

- Require collateral when you extend credit to a customer so that you become a secured creditor if that customer develops serious business problems.

- Monitor the industry conditions of your customer groups to stay attuned to slowdowns and other developments that may affect your customers' ability to pay on a timely basis so that you can adjust your credit policies accordingly.

- Monitor the financial condition of your individual customers so that you can anticipate problems and make necessary adjustments.

---

**Survival Tip #28**

**Consider consulting with the credit manager of a company similar to yours for tips on managing receivables. Or, call the National Association of Credit Management, (410) 740-5560, for information on effective credit management.**

---

## Creditors, Bankers and Suppliers

It is always best to meet with creditors, bankers and suppliers as soon as cash flow projections or other financial data point to the likelihood of financial problems. Early meetings will assure everyone that you are on top of your business, which will make them more comfortable about helping you address your problems. Another advantage of early meetings is that creditors, bankers and suppliers will have more options for helping you.

If you wait too long to deal with your problems, your creditors, bankers and suppliers, like your employees, will probably already be aware of your situation. More than likely, you will already have experienced trouble meeting your financial obligations. As a result, those you owe money to may be growing nervous, unsure of what you are planning to do about the problems and concerned that you may try to avoid paying them entirely. Since in most cases the cooperation of your creditors will be essential to your ability to successfully deal with your business's difficulties, do not do anything that is going to encourage those creditors to begin making defensive moves that could exacerbate your problems or jeopardize your chances for resolving them. Do not avoid creditor phone calls or fail to respond to their letters, and do not lie to them. If any of your creditors contact you, acknowledge that you are having difficulties but that you are taking steps to stabilize your situation and ask for their patience. Creditors, suppliers and bankers who feel that you are not dealing effectively with your problems are apt to be less amenable to making the financial concessions you may need from them.

---

## Survival Tip #29

**Never keep money in a bank to which you owe money. That way, if the bank begins to feel uncomfortable about your business, it cannot raid your account without telling you so. This will also help you avoid writing hot checks because you were unaware of the bank's raid.**

---

## Gaining Financial Concessions

When faced with financial problems, an important component of most business game plans involves getting your suppliers, creditors and bankers to agree to certain financial concessions. These concessions, usually necessary to increase cash flow and stabilize your business, might include:

- revising debt repayment plans to lower monthly payments and to extend the period of repayment;
- refinancing; and
- arranging for interest-only payments on a debt for a specified period of time.

Concessions should be proposed in one-on-one meetings with the appropriate parties whenever possible, not by phone or in a letter.

## *Meeting with the Banker*

*The banker had John W.'s business future in his hands. All the profits from John's small trucking firm were going to the bank on a note used to buy more trucks.*

*John and I met with his banker to discuss restructuring the note, something that was necessary if John's company was going to survive. The fact that I was in attendance and that the banker knew I represented debtors in the bankruptcy process helped him realize what was likely to happen if his bank was not willing to work with John's business. I was not there to threaten the banker—I was there to help demonstrate that it was in the bank's best interest to work with John.*

*John and I came to the meeting prepared with photographs of the bank's collateral that illustrated its present condition. We also brought to the meeting an appraiser who demonstrated that the bank would lose money if it repossessed and sold the collateral.*

*Financial projections for John's business showed a reduction in monthly payments to the bank along with a plan to sell some of the trucks to reduce the total amount of debt to the bank, all of which would help the business survive. We also explained to the banker how reductions in overhead would be achieved through staff cuts.*

*John was lucky; his business was ultimately able to avoid bankruptcy due to the help of his banker. Key to John's success was the time he spent preparing a well-thought-out game plan for resolving his financial problems, backed up with financial projections and other documentation. However, John might have been able to avoid the threat of bankruptcy and the time and hassle of preparing for the meeting if he had done a better job of monitoring his business's financial situation and identified problems early in their development.*

Before setting up meetings with creditors, be sure that you have prepared a realistic, workable game plan and that you have also developed a well-thought-out strategy for dealing with each creditor, banker or supplier. Figure 4.2 contains tips for successful meetings with creditors, bankers and suppliers. When developing your strategies, do not hesitate to seek help from your professional advisors, trusted business associates or bankruptcy attorney.

**Figure 4.2   Tips for Successful Meetings with Creditors, Bankers and Suppliers**

Although there are no foolproof 100 percent guaranteed strategies for successful negotiations, here are a few tips that can increase the likelihood of your success:

- Remain calm and reasonable.

- Be clear before you go to your meetings about the exact message you want to convey and what you are asking for.

- Identify any background information, industry-related research, financial data, etc. that will strengthen your position, and provide copies as leave-behinds.

- Talk to your creditors and bankers in terms of their interest, not yours.

- Remember that your creditors and bankers extended you credit because they wanted to make money.

- If possible, negotiate in person, not by letter or telephone.

## Survival Tip #30

**Always try to meet with your creditors and bankers individually. Otherwise, you risk having your bargaining ability undermined by the strength of the group.**

You do not need to treat everyone alike in your game plan. Your strategies should reflect the relative importance to your business of each creditor, banker and supplier, as well as a recognition of who could do the most damage to your company if they were to take action against you. Then, work hardest to gain the cooperation of the most important or the most potentially dangerous.

## Survival Tip #31

**Do not overlook the IRS! It is an extremely powerful creditor and should be at the top of your list.**

Prior to a meeting, know exactly what you will ask for and the argument that you will use to convince those in attendance that your proposal is reasonable. Always frame your argument in terms of how your proposal will benefit your audience. Be prepared for the possibility that you will not get exactly what you want or that your first proposal may be denied. Have at least one fall-back position in mind, and know exactly what you are willing to give up or compromise on to get what you need.

Each meeting should have two goals. Your first goal should be to gain some breathing space—to take some of the pressure off—by getting creditors, bankers and suppliers to agree to changes and concessions that will increase your monthly cash flow. That will buy you time to sort out your situation and stabilize your finances.

---

### Survival Tip #32

**In your anxiety to gain additional cash to fund your business or to restructure existing credit, be careful about signing personal guarantees. If you do, you place your personal assets at risk. Get legal advice before doing so.**

---

Your second goal should be to make your creditors, bankers and suppliers part of your team. Do this by convincing them that you have a workable strategy for resolving your financial problems and stabilizing your business. As Adam Radzick warns, "This (when a business is in crisis) is not a time to be secretive and protective, but a time to actually open up your situation to the people who are in effect your financial partners, and to ask them for their help." When necessary, provide your creditors with cash flow and sales projections, fact sheets and documentation that will help support your case.

During each meeting, honestly lay out your situation, demonstrate that you have a good understanding of your business's problems and explain the solutions you have in mind. Clearly state your needs and explain why the group's help will make a difference. Whenever possible, establish some specific goals and benchmarks that your creditors can use to evaluate the effectiveness of your recovery efforts and to monitor your progress.

## Once an Agreement Is Negotiated

If your negotiations are successful, maintain the confidence of your creditors, bankers and suppliers by meeting regularly with each of them. These meetings will help demonstrate that you are doing what you said you would do.

Also at these meetings, take advantage of the expertise of your creditors, bankers and suppliers by asking them for their advice and input. They may have excellent, workable ideas and, because they are involved in your industry, they may have connections and information that could be of help.

## New Sources of Cash

Most financially troubled businesses need additional cash to survive once their situation has stabilized and started to turn around. Cash may be needed to catch up with financial obligations, to purchase new inventory, to add staff or to pay for other activities necessary to a business's long-term recovery and stability. Although some of this cash can be raised by slashing expenses and increasing sales, these measures alone may not be enough. You will need additional outside capital from institutional sources.

Locating adequate outside capital can be a major problem for even a healthy small business, so it can be especially difficult for the business that is coping with problems. Therefore, the search for additional capital should begin as soon as possible.

---

### Survival Tip #33

**An overly long delay in finding outside capital can retard and even destroy your business's improvement.**

---

Before searching for outside capital, be sure that you have exhausted all internal opportunities for generating additional cash so you minimize the amount of outside capital you need. Most lenders or investors will want you to demonstrate to them that you have maximized the productivity of all assets, slashed expenses and done everything else possible to generate additional cash flow before they will consider working with you. Here are some additional cash-generating possibilities to consider:

- Cut expenses to the bone.
- Borrow against your accounts receivables. The usual advance will be up to 80 percent of the value of your receivables, but your bank will base its lending decision on the strength of your receivables and your business's overall financial condition.
- Rent out office, warehouse or plant space that you do not need.
- When not using it, offer others the use of your equipment on a contract basis—evenings, weekends, slow times, etc.
- Keep less inventory on hand.
- Identify other ways to use your assets when they are not being used by your primary business.
- Barter for services.
- Sell selected assets, and lease them back.
- Make greater use of free-lancers and independent contractors.
- Cash in investments.
- Increase the price of your products or services especially if you can add—for little or no cost—a corollary product or service with a perceived benefit to your customers.
- Take advantage of your recognized expertise or skill in a certain area, and develop a new product or service based on it that requires little or no additional expenditure of money, additional marketing, etc.
- Explore the possibility of a joint venture with a company in a similar or complimentary business to yours. For example, perhaps you and another company can enter into an arrangement whereby you manufacture a product for cash up front, and the other company handles distribution and marketing with an agreement to take its share of the proceeds at the end of the manufacturing and sales process.
- If you have not already done so, consult with outside professionals, such as representatives of SCORE or the SBA, as well as with your accountant, bankruptcy attorney or another reputable professional who may be able to provide you with ideas and advice.

In difficult times, Adam Radzick urges business owners to be creative by exploring every opportunity to make better use of their business's assets. If, despite its difficulties, a business still has a customer base, Radzick suggests that the business may be able to refine or retool an existing product or service to make it more responsive to customer needs or wants. Or, by analyzing company skills and abilities and adapting them to changes in the market- place, Radzick suggests that a small business owner may be able to redefine its product or service, opening up new markets for itself or strengthening its position in its current market.

---

### Survival Tip #34

**Be innovative. Brainstorm with trusted advisors about new uses or markets for your products/services and about new ways that your tangible and intangible assets can be used. Read industry publications to learn about ways that others in your industry are innovating.**

---

One additional option is to put more of your own money, or the money of friends and relatives, into your business. However, do not do this unless you have a very clear understanding of your business's financial health and are confident of its long-term prog- nosis. Also, don't put more of your own money in if you don't understand exactly how much your business needs each month to keep its doors open. If the amount you or friends and family would put into the business is just a drop in the bucket compared to what is needed, it is probably not advisable to pass the bucket.

---

### Survival Tip #35

**Always secure loans from relatives with collateral so that if you later file bankruptcy, they will be in a better position than other creditors.**

---

## Sources of Institutional Capital

Before you begin approaching possible sources of institutional capital, your business's financial situation must have stabilized. Banks, venture capital firms, etc. are in business to make money.

They will not work with you if they believe that you are at the helm of a sinking ship. Such groups also will be reluctant to work with you if they:

- believe that your business is fundamentally flawed;
- have concerns about your business's management; or
- doubt the long-term potential of your business.

When searching for sources of capital, it is a good idea to start with the funding sources you've already worked with and know well. Your logical first stop is your current bank, especially if you have taken the time to establish a good relationship with your loan officer. However, it is a good idea to apply to other banks at the same time.

## Survival Tip #36

**Avoid loan brokers whenever possible, since these middlemen will charge you a percentage of the loan's total amount. Some brokers will demand money up front and then fail to find you a loan.**

Venture capital financing is another possibility, although it is a long shot. Another option is to approach a larger firm that is in the same business as yours and discuss a mutually beneficial financial arrangement. For example, a larger company might invest in your business or purchase a percentage of it.

If you locate an investor who is interested in putting a substantial amount of money into your business, the investor may expect to become your partner in order to protect the investment. However, this arrangement has its downside, especially if you are a sole proprietor. In a partnership, you are 100 percent liable for all partnership liabilities, even if you do not incur them yourself. Therefore, before entering into such an arrangement, weigh carefully its potential risks and benefits and learn as much as possible about the background and business habits of your potential partner.

If you do find someone who would like to put money into your business, a better option is to treat the investment as a loan and draw up an agreement for collateral and regular payments. Or, set up a corporation, making you and the investor shareholders and stockholders. This way you will be shielded from any liabilities the investor might create.

Other possible sources of capital include the SBA and your local or state business development agency. However, working with government agencies can be time-consuming and require a lot of paperwork—you may experience a long delay before you actually get your money. Also, commercial finance companies sometimes will lend money to a small business that is recovering from financial problems, albeit at a high rate of interest. Commercial finance companies are sometimes willing to extend money against strong accounts receivables.

## If Your Financial Problems Worsen

If your business problems fail to improve despite your efforts, reread the previous sections of this chapter to see if you have overlooked any possible action. Consider pursuing measures you've not already taken and revisiting those you've already taken to determine if you can do more in those areas. If you have not already done so, schedule a meeting with a reputable bankruptcy attorney. If you had visited a bankruptcy attorney at the outset of your efforts to develop and implement an effective plan of action, schedule a follow-up meeting.

You may also want to consult again with trusted advisors. They can view your situation more objectively than you can and may be better able to recognize when things are hopeless and it is time to close your doors or declare bankruptcy. Another option, if you have the resources and feel that you have done all you can, is to consult with a turnaround specialist.

## Turnaround Specialists

Turnaround specialists are professionals who help financially troubled companies avoid bankruptcy. A skilled, experienced specialist can be a lifesaver to the business with sufficient resources to use such a service and is an appropriate resource for the business in crisis. Although most turnaround specialists work with larger firms, some work with small businesses.

## Survival Tip #37

**To locate a turnaround specialist in your area, talk with your attorney, banker or accountant. Also, consider contacting the Chicago-based Turnaround Management Association, (312) 879-2124.**

Most specialists require money up front to begin working with you. Additionally, most are paid a monthly retainer plus expenses. However, if cash is in short supply and the chances for a successful turnaround are strong, some specialists will enter into an equity payment relationship with a company whereby they take a percentage of ownership in return for not charging an up-front fee and retainer.

## Survival Tip #38

**A responsible turnaround specialist will not charge huge fees and expenses that can choke a business. If the proposed charges of the specialist you are talking with seem too high, look for another.**

Turnaround specialists do the following:

- Marshal resources to enhance the likelihood that a business will survive.
- Focus first on the areas of a business that are hemorrhaging.
- Utilize a business's resources more effectively and productively in order to effect a turnaround

According to Adam Radzick, "The turnaround specialist should as quickly as possible, identify the areas of greatest hemorrhage in a business; and he should be sticking his fingers and hands and feet and everything else he can find into that hole in the dike."

### *The Advantages of Working with a Turnaround Specialist*

Working with a seasoned, capable turnaround specialist has several important advantages. First, as objective outsiders with experience working with financially troubled businesses, these professionals are adept at quickly diagnosing a business's problems, analyzing its options and developing and implementing an effective plan that stops the immediate effects of the problems.

Second, turnaround specialists are usually better than the average business owner at doing what needs to be done to save a business. In part, this is because turnaround specialists have no emotional attachments to the business, its products or services or its employees. Therefore, these specialists can very pragmatically slash expenses, cut payroll and do whatever else is necessary to raise cash quickly and to save the business.

Third, because they have experience negotiating with creditors and bankers, turnaround specialists are better able than the average small business person to work out revised debt payment plans or other financial concessions that will benefit the struggling business. Sometimes the mere fact that you have hired a turnaround specialist can bolster the trust and confidence of your creditors, bankers and suppliers in your ability to weather your difficulties. The hiring of a turnaround specialist signals to your creditors that you are serious about resolving your situation.

Fourth, seasoned turnaround specialists are adept at playing *good guy, bad guy* at the appropriate points in the negotiation process—they know when to hold their cards close to their chest and when to lay them on the table. Consequently, turnaround specialists are better able to manipulate the negotiations to the advantage of the business.

Fifth, a turnaround specialist will know of potential sources of outside capital and which are most apt to loan money to a business.

## The Characteristics of an Effective Turnaround Specialist

As in every profession, there are good and bad turnaround specialists. If you feel that you can afford the services of a professional, be sure that the turnaround specialist you choose:

- has been working in the profession for at least five years;
- has specific experience working with businesses in your industry;
- is a problem solver, a planner and an implementer;
- believes that a successful turnaround requires a partnership with the business owner and wants to utilize the skills and knowledge of the owner; and

- demonstrates respect for you as the business owner, but is willing to challenge your assumptions and attitudes and question your perspectives.

## Conclusion

If your business experiences financial difficulties, prompt and decisive action is required. You must diagnose the cause of your difficulties, implement actions that will alleviate the effects of those difficulties and develop a game plan for constructive action so that your business problems do not recur. Possible actions include adjustments to your management systems or operations, staff changes, reductions in expenses, negotiations with creditors, bankers and suppliers, the development of new markets, a redefinition of your product or service, or locating additional capital. Another option may be bankruptcy.

However you decide to deal with your financial problems, your actions should be based on a careful analysis of your financial records and projections as well as an assessment of your competition and current and projected market conditions. It is also advisable to seek the advice of outside professionals including your accountant and a bankruptcy attorney. A bankruptcy attorney can help you assess the seriousness of your situation and may be able to provide you with information that can help you avoid bankruptcy. If you have the funds to do so, hiring a turnaround specialist—a professional who helps financially troubled businesses survive—is another excellent way to deal with serious business problems.

# The IRS and Payroll Taxes

*T*rouble with the IRS is a common source of serious financial difficulty for countless small businesses. Typically, that difficulty is the result of businesses failing to meet their payroll tax obligations.

Getting behind on payroll taxes can be the kiss of death for a small business. Until a business's tax liability is paid in full, the IRS will charge interest (somewhat higher than the market rate) compounded daily, on the unpaid balance, as well as penalties. In addition, interest will be assessed on the unpaid balance of penalties and interest. If a small business is unwilling or unable to voluntarily take care of its delinquent taxes, the IRS will take enforced collection action to collect its money.

Because payroll tax problems can be financially devastating to a business and sometimes to its owner as well, *The Small Business Survival Kit* devotes three chapters to the IRS and payroll taxes. As a starting point, in this chapter, I provide an overview of the IRS collection process, including a discussion of the role of Revenue Officers and the Trust Fund Recovery Penalty. Additionally, I explain the IRS definition and concept of *responsible persons* and how that affects collection proceedings. Major reasons for the development of payroll tax problems and tips for avoiding such problems are provided, and the options available to businesses who get behind on their payroll taxes are reviewed.

## Payroll Taxes Defined

Payroll taxes are the dollars that a business with one or more employees is obligated to collect and pay to the IRS. These taxes include federal income taxes, Social Security and Medicare. A business is responsible for collecting a portion of the taxes through employee payroll tax deductions. The money deducted from employees' paychecks is referred to as *trust fund tax dollars*. Businesses are also obligated to match some of the employee payroll deductions with their own dollars. All payroll tax monies are supposed to be deposited with an authorized financial institution. Employers are required to use the funds to make periodic payroll tax payments to the IRS.

---

### Survival Tip #39

**If you have questions about payroll taxes or other federal tax-related questions, call the IRS office listed in your local phone directory under the federal government listings, or call the agency at (800) 829-1040.**

---

The IRS holds a very negative view of any business that fails to pay its payroll taxes on time and in full since such businesses are not meeting their federal tax obligations. The agency particularly frowns on businesses that make employee payroll tax deductions but then use the money to pay their business expenses instead of depositing payroll taxes until it is time to pay the IRS. In essence, the IRS views this as nothing more than stealing employees' money.

## An Overview of the IRS Collection Process

Once the IRS identifies a business that owes at least one quarter of back payroll taxes, it will send the business a series of notices intended to encourage it to voluntarily pay its tax liability. These notices will inform the delinquent business that its taxes are immediately due in full and will let the business know that interest is accruing.

The IRS also will inform a tax delinquent business about any penalties it may be assessed. These penalties can include:

- failure to deposit;
- failure to file; and
- failure to pay.

In determining the amount and type of penalties to assess, the IRS will consider the business's specific violations as well as other factors. These factors may include the length of time that the taxes have been delinquent, the reason for the delinquency and the business's history with the IRS.

---

## Survival Tip #40

**Do not ignore any notice from the IRS. Make the agency your number one priority! If you don't, your debt will increase and your options for resolving your tax problems will decrease.**

---

If a business does not have the money to pay the full amount of its tax liability, the IRS may allow the business to clear up its debt through an installment payment plan. An *Offer in Compromise* may be another option. Both options are discussed in Chapter 6.

If a business ignores the IRS notices, or if the agency does not allow the business to use an installment plan or an Offer in Compromise, it is likely that the IRS will pursue the use of enforced collection actions, such as seizure and sale, levies or liens in order to get its money. These actions can be devastating to a small business.

---

## Survival Tip #41

**The IRS gets its tax dollars in approximately 90 percent of all delinquent tax cases!**

---

### Lack of IRS Resources

Most IRS offices lack adequate staffing levels and the other resources needed to do an efficient job of identifying businesses with payroll tax problems soon after those problems develop. As a result, delays in contacting a business about its taxes often mean that the business has developed a very large tax liability by the time it finally hears from the IRS. Frequently this liability is so substantial that the business's only real option for dealing with the debt is to file for bankruptcy.

---

## Survival Tip #42

**It can take as long as two years before a business will ever be contacted by the IRS about delinquent payroll taxes.**

---

These long delays can have other effects as well. They can actually encourage some business owners to avoid recognizing that they have a tax problem and to refrain from doing something about it. Sometimes this means that a business that is using payroll tax dollars as operating capital remains in business with its tax liability growing far longer than it would if it were contacted by the IRS soon after the first signs of trouble.

IRS delays can actually encourage some business owners to knowingly misuse payroll tax dollars. If a business doesn't hear from the IRS soon after it fails to pay its taxes and uses the funds for other expenses instead, some business owners will foolishly begin to think they never will hear from the IRS.

### Determination of Responsible Persons

When the IRS identifies a business with delinquent payroll taxes, it not only sends the business a series of notices in order to affect voluntary payment of the tax liability, it also tries to identify the person(s) responsible for the delinquency. Once that is determined, the IRS will assess a trust fund recovery penalty against each *responsible person*.

The IRS considers a responsible person to be someone who was aware that the taxes were not paid and who used the funds for other purposes or directed that they be used for other purposes. For example, if your business is experiencing cash flow problems and you decided to use trust fund dollars to pay the utility bill rather than the IRS, you would be considered a responsible person.

When assigning responsibility, the IRS will pay special attention to anyone who has the authority to sign checks for the business, who makes financial decisions for a business, or who has responsibility for the financial operations of a business.

A responsible person may be:

- a sole proprietor, partner or a corporate officer;
- a corporate director or a shareholder;
- an employee; or
- anyone with enough control over a company's funds to direct disbursement.

The IRS also may define as responsible someone not directly associated with a business who furnished the business with funds and directed the use of those funds.

## Survival Tip #43

**If you delegate signatory responsibility for your business's payroll taxes to a bookkeeper, you are still responsible for the taxes.**

## *The Trust Fund Recovery Penalty*

The IRS will assess a trust fund recovery penalty equal to 100 percent of a business's unpaid trust fund taxes against each responsible person and the full amount of the past due trust fund taxes will become the *personal* tax liability of each of them. Responsible persons will receive a tax bill and a notice from their IRS District Office. This penalty will be assessed even if the delinquent business is no longer operating and has no assets.

## Survival Tip #44

**The IRS can recover unpaid trust fund tax dollars by automatically applying the personal income tax refund of a responsible person to a business's tax liability.**

If a business fails to clear up its tax debt, the IRS will initiate collection actions against each responsible person. A responsible person can pay the debt in full or can work out an installment plan or Offer in Compromise. If a responsible person ignores the tax liability, the IRS may initiate enforced collection actions against him or her.

### *The Appeals Process*

If at any point during the collection process, a business or a responsible person disagrees with an IRS decision—about the amount of taxes owed, the amount and type of penalties assessed, designation of the responsible persons, the terms of an installment agreement, etc.—it can appeal the decision. Some businesses also use the appeals process to buy themselves time to deal with the IRS or simply to delay the inevitable.

---

### Survival Tip #45

**While an IRS decision is being appealed, interest and penalties will continue to mount.**

---

If a business does not get satisfaction through the appeals process, it can also sue the agency in federal court. The particular court you sue in will depend upon whether or not you pay the taxes in dispute before going to court.

Once an appeal is filed, a hearing will be scheduled. Before the date of the hearing, be sure you have gathered and reviewed any documentation that supports your position.

---

### Survival Tip #46

**If you are considering an appeal, contact the IRS, your lawyer or accountant to find out if there are time limitations on the filing of an appeal or other considerations.**

---

It is not unusual for an IRS appeals officer to rule in favor of a business. This is because IRS officers are under pressure to be certain that if an appeal is denied and the business takes the IRS to court, there is a strong likelihood that the IRS will prevail. Therefore, if there are any weak spots in the agency's position, the appeals officer is apt to side with the business rather than risk an IRS loss in court.

## Survival Tip #47

**If the court determines that an IRS decision was "largely unjustified," you may be able to recover some of your administrative and litigation costs. However, you must have pursued all administrative remedies prior to taking the IRS to court.**

## *The IRS Revenue Officer*

Once a business is identified as tax delinquent, the IRS will assign a revenue officer to help the business expediently resolve its tax delinquency and attempt to collect as much of the back taxes as possible.

Much of a business's experience with the IRS will be shaped by its relationship with the revenue officer. Therefore, it is important that you understand a little about these IRS professionals and how best to work with them. Figure 5.1 summarizes tips for establishing a good relationship with your revenue officer.

Most revenue officers are reasonably well-educated, dedicated to their jobs and serious about what they do. They also tend to be extremely overworked and under pressure and enjoy considerable decision-making authority in carrying out their responsibilities.

There is, however, a wide disparity among revenue officers in regard to their abilities and skills and their approach to their work. Some are very enforcement-minded and tend to interpret IRS rules and regulations quite literally. Others are easier to work with, assuming you are not a blatant tax delinquent or evader, and are more open to compromise.

**Figure 5.1   Tips for Developing a Successful Relationship with Your Revenue Officer**

A positive relationship with a revenue officer can make it much easier for you to resolve your tax problems. Harvey Corn, a CPA based in Austin, Texas, offers these tips for developing a smooth working relationship with an officer:

- Don't be defensive about your tax problems or use the IRS as a scapegoat. Let the officer know you are ready to help the IRS collect its taxes. An "I'm willing to cooperate fully" attitude is more apt to win concessions from the IRS than a hostile, chip-on-your-shoulder demeanor.

- Be calm and reasonable when you disagree with the revenue officer.

- Meet all deadlines. When the revenue officer requests information, get it to him or her by the established deadline.

- Never miss a deadline without letting the revenue officer know well in advance.

- If the revenue officer phones and you miss the call, return the call as soon as you can.

- Prior to your initial meeting with the revenue officer, complete all necessary paperwork and bring it to the meeting. This will help convey that you are serious about cooperating with the IRS and that you want to make the process as easy as possible.

## Lost Temper, Lost Cause

*I knew I was going to have trouble with Jim A., a potential client, as soon as he sat in my office explaining that the IRS had no right to take insurance sale commissions to satisfy his payroll tax delinquency. Jim was angry and wanted to know what he could do about the situation.*

*When I explained to Jim that the IRS had every right to do what it was doing, his disappointment was obvious. I reviewed his options and suggested that he contact an accountant friend of mine who specializes in working out IRS installment plans for businesses.*

*A month later, the accountant called to say that he was sending Jim back to me so that I could file a reorganization bankruptcy. I was surprised; Jim's tax troubles hadn't seemed serious enough to merit bankruptcy.*

*The accountant explained, "I took Jim with me to the IRS office because the revenue officer wanted to review some documents." By the time the meeting was over, Jim had done everything he could to insult the officer; he was so angry I thought he was going to fly across the desk and attack her! I literally dragged Jim out into the hall and tried to calm him down but to no avail. Jim's anger ruined any chance we had for a negotiated settlement."*

*I decided to pass on representing Jim. Some people are unable to resolve their problems with the IRS because their anger gets in the way.*

## Misuse of Payroll Tax Monies

Many businesses get into trouble with the IRS because when money is tight they do not deposit the payroll tax dollars they are obligated to pay the agency. Instead, they use the funds to meet immediate cash needs, gambling that when it's time to pay the agency, they'll be able to come up with the money.

That gamble is very risky. More often than not, the business will find that it is unable to catch up on its taxes and that it falls further and further behind.

Other business owners are so busy generating new business and taking care of day-to-day business activities that they forget to collect their payroll taxes or to pay them on time.

## Survival Tip #48

**If you are an absentee business owner or a silent partner in a business and have either delegated payroll responsibilities to an employee or to the partner who is actively involved in the operation of the partnership, protect yourself by requiring regular proof that the taxes have been paid.**

Sole proprietorships and businesspeople who are the sole shareholders in a corporation can develop payroll tax problems in another way—by taking draws from their business as a salary and not deducting payroll taxes from the amount they receive. If they do this, they may find that when April 15 arrives, they are faced with a personal income tax bill they cannot pay. These unpaid taxes can spell TROUBLE for both the business owner and the business.

## Employee Misclassifications

Some small businesses develop payroll tax problems because they misclassify workers as independent contractors and consequently fail to collect and pay payroll taxes for these workers. Often this misclassification occurs because the business does not clearly understand the criteria used by the IRS to distinguish between employees and independent contractors.

Sometimes, however, employee misclassification is a deliberate action on the part of a less-than-scrupulous business to reduce its costs since employers are not required to collect or pay payroll taxes for an independent contractor. Also, the IRS has fewer reporting requirements for independent contractors than for employees, so there is less paperwork involved with them. Employers must file quarterly reports on each employee. For independent contractors, however, the IRS only requires an employer to file a Form 1099 once a year.

If the IRS discovers that a business has been misclassifying its employees, the business will have to pay its back payroll taxes.

### Distinctions Between Independent Contractors and Employees

In very general terms, an independent contractor is a self-employed worker who is usually hired on an hourly or project basis. Typically, such persons are paid by the job, provide their own equipment and tools, hire their own assistants and work for multiple companies.

The IRS uses a list of 20 criteria that employers should use as guidelines to help them distinguish between an employee and an independent contractor. For example, it classifies a worker as an employee if the worker's time is controlled by the business, i.e., the employer determines the number of hours a person works as well as what that person will do during those hours. The IRS also considers a worker to be an employee if the person is hired and trained by the business and supervised at the employer's place of business in exchange for wages. See Figure 5.2 for a complete list of IRS guidelines.

**Figure 5.2    Employee or Independent Contractor? IRS Guidelines**

---

The IRS has established 20 guidelines to help employers determine whether a worker should be treated as an employee or an independent contractor for tax purposes. Those 20 guidelines are:

1. *Instructions.*   Employees comply with their employer's instructions about when, where and how to work, or the employer has the right to control how a worker's work results are achieved. Independent contractors have more flexibility.

2. *Training.*   Employees may receive training from their employers to perform services in a particular manner. Independent contractors usually use their own work methods and receive no training from those purchasing their services.

3. *Integration.*   Employees' services are usually integrated into the business's operations because they are key to the success or the continuation of the business. Independent contractors are independent of the business's operation.

4. *Services Rendered Personally.*   Employees render services personally. Independent contractors render services as contractors.

5. *Hiring Assistants.*   Employees work for an employer. Independent contractors can hire, supervise and pay assistants under a contract that requires them to provide materials and labor and to be responsible for the results.

6. *Continuing Relationship.*   Employees generally have ongoing relationships with their employers. Independent contractors' relationships will usually be more sporadic.

7. *Set Hours of Work.*   Employers usually set their employees' work hours. Independent contractors usually set their own hours.

8. *Full-Time Required.*   Employees may be required to work or to be available full-time. Independent contractors may work when and for whom they choose.

9. *Work Done on Premises.*   Employees usually work on their employers' premises or on a route or at a location approved by their employers.

10. *Order or Sequence Set.*   Employees may be required to perform services in the order or sequence set by their employers. Independent contractors can establish their own sequence.

**Figure 5.2   Employee or Independent Contractor? IRS Guidelines (Continued)**

11. *Reports.*   Employees may be required to submit reports to their employers. Independent contractors are not required to submit reports to their clients.

12. *Payments.*   Employees are paid by the hour, week or month. Independent contractors are usually paid by the job or through a commission.

13. *Expenses.*   The business and travel expenses of employees are generally paid by their employers. Independent contractors are responsible for paying their own expenses.

14. *Tools and Materials.*   Employers normally furnish their employees with the key tools, materials and other materials they need to do their jobs. Independent contractors normally furnish their own tools and materials.

15. *Investment.*   Employees normally do not invest in the facilities. Independent contractors have a significant investment in the facilities they use to perform services for someone else.

16. *Profit and Loss.*   Employees do not experience a profit or loss; independent contractors can.

17. *Works for More Than One Person or Firm.*   Employees usually work for one firm at a time. Independent contractors may work for multiple persons or firms at the same time.

18. *Offers Services to the General Public.*   Employees usually work for one employer. Independent contractors make their services available to whomever they want.

19. *Right to Fire.*   Employees can be fired by their employers. Independent contractors cannot be fired as long as they produce a result that meets the specifications of their contract.

20. *Right to Quit.*   Employees have the right to quit a job at any time without incurring liability. Independent contractors usually agree to carry out specific tasks or series of tasks and are responsible for completing those tasks satisfactorily, or are legally obligated to make good for failing to do so.

If you have questions about these guidelines, call the IRS office closest to you.

Most workers in this country are appropriately classified as employees, not independent contractors. In fact, out of the entire U.S. work force, only about eight percent of workers can qualify as independent contractors.

## Survival Tip #49

*IRS Publication 937, Employment Taxes and Information Returns* **describes in detail how to determine the appropriate classification for a worker. If after reading it you still have questions, call the IRS or ask that the agency do the classifying for you by filing a Form SS-8,** *Determination of Employee Work Status.*

## How the IRS Discovers an Employee Misclassification

There are a number of ways that the IRS can discover an employee misclassification, including:

- A worker makes a formal or an informal complaint to the IRS that his or her employer is not making payroll tax deductions.
- The IRS reviews a business's tax returns and notes the possibility of a misclassification.
- The revenue officer assigned to a business with payroll tax problems suspects that employees have been misclassified and refers the company to the IRS office that investigates possible misclassifications.

## IRS Investigation of a Possible Classification Problem

If the IRS suspects that employees are being misclassified, it will conduct an investigation. The agency will review applicable paperwork and tax returns to see if there has been a change in the pattern of a company's withholding practices and may also talk to the business owner to learn the basis for the classifications. The agency will also compare the business to industry standards.

If the IRS discovers misclassification problems, it will assess the degree and the frequency of the noncompliance. And, the IRS will also determine whether the misclassification was intentional. This may involve interviews with business owners and employees as well.

### *Unintentional Misclassifications*

If the IRS decides that misclassifications were unintentional, the business will be held fully responsible for the employer portion of the taxes that should have been paid if the worker had been appropriately classified. In addition, the business will be liable for a nominal percentage of the unpaid trust fund taxes.

### *Intentional Misclassifications*

The IRS will deal more harshly with a business that it believes is deliberately misclassifying workers. It will make the business liable for all of the payroll taxes it should have paid.

---

### Survival Tip #50

**The IRS will be less amenable to an installment agreement or an Offer in Compromise when it believes that misclassifications are deliberate.**

---

### *What To Do When Payroll Tax Problems Develop*

Regardless of the reason for payroll tax problems, the fundamental solution is always the same—as quickly as possible, identify why the problems exist, do everything you can to get current on your taxes and prevent future payroll tax problems. See Figure 5.3 for advice on avoiding payroll tax problems.

Here are some questions you should be asking yourself:

- Am I having problems because I am not doing a good job of managing my business?
- Does my business use payroll tax dollars as operating capital? In other words, could I continue to operate if I weren't subsidizing my business with tax dollars?
- Do I forget to pay my taxes, or do I avoid dealing with them because I think they're a hassle?
- Do I clearly understand the difference between an employee and an independent contractor?
- Are there steps I can take to address the reasons for my payroll tax problems? What are the costs of these steps and how quickly will I see their benefits?

**Figure 5.3   How To Avoid Payroll Tax Problems**

Here are important rules of thumb to avoid payroll tax problems:

- Use payroll tax dollars *only* to meet tax obligations.

- Pay the taxes in full when they are due.

- Do not misclassify employees.

- Hire a bookkeeper or a payroll tax service to handle payroll taxes.

- Deposit tax moneys with an authorized financial institution each pay period rather than each quarter in order to reduce the temptation to use the money for other purposes.

- Talk with your accountant or another trusted business advisor about things you can do to increase your business's efficiency and profitability.

## *Expensive Shortcuts*

*I should have guessed that Billy O. owned a barbecue stand when he entered my office. He carried all of his records in brown paper sacks and a wonderful smoky aroma surrounded him.*

*Although Billy had a great product and was doing well, he had no interest in the details of running a business. For example, because he did not like bookkeeping and did not use the services of a bookkeeper, he had been treating all of his employees as independent contractors. That way Billy didn't have to calculate payroll tax deductions or worry about making payroll tax deposits.*

*Unfortunately, however, after years of running his business this way, the IRS had caught up with Billy. Now this small businessman was looking at a tax liability of more than $80,000! Ultimately, to get out of hot water with the IRS, Billy sold all the real estate he had accumulated over the years and hired an outside bookkeeper to handle his payroll taxes.*

## Conclusion

It is always best to pay all your taxes in full and on time. That way you will avoid the paperwork and hassle of dealing with the IRS, and you will not incur the additional expense of interest and penalties and the possibility of legal expenses as well. However, as this chapter points out, many small businesses develop problems with the IRS.

If your analysis of your business indicates that it is viable and you want to remain in business despite your tax problems, your first step should be to determine whether or not you can come up with the cash you need to immediately wipe out your debt. Possible sources of funds include: borrowed money, the liquidation of unencumbered business assets and the sale of personal assets. However, if you do not have access to these sources of funds or if they are not enough to cover your tax debt, you should contact the IRS about the possibility of an installment plan or an Offer in Compromise. Both of these options are discussed in detail in the following chapter.

Another option for dealing with a debt to the IRS when you want to remain in business is to file a Chapter 13 or Chapter 11 reorganization bankruptcy. To understand when this option is appropriate, read Chapters 9, 11 and 12.

If your business analysis indicates that your business is not viable or if you no longer want to be in business, you need to consider the best way to close down. Chapter 8 provides an overview of your options while Chapters 9 and 10 discuss the use of a Chapter 7 liquidation bankruptcy as a means of shutting down. Be sure to read Chapter 6 as well so that you have a full understanding of the possible ways that you can pay off your debt to the IRS if a lump sum payment is not possible.

Whatever you do, when you are having problems with the IRS, do not avoid dealing with them or you will face the very serious enforced collection actions outlined in Chapter 7. Instead, it is best to take decisive action to resolve your IRS problems. Before doing so, read all relevant chapters in this book, and consult with your accountant and a bankruptcy attorney to ensure that you have a complete understanding of your situation and your options in order to make the best choice.

# IRS Installment Plans and Offers in Compromise

*T*wo options for clearing up a debt with the IRS are installment payment plans and Offers in Compromise. In this chapter, I will review when each option is appropriate, how the options work and under what conditions the IRS will allow them. Tips for working with the IRS to get a payment arrangement approved as well as advice about selecting a professional to deal with the IRS on your behalf are also included.

An installment plan gives a business the opportunity to clear up its IRS debt through regular monthly payments.

**Survival Tip #51**

**You will be expected to use an installment plan to clear up your tax debt if the IRS feels that you are capable of paying your debt in full. If due to your age, income, health or some other limiting factor, an installment plan is not possible, the IRS will consider an Offer in Compromise.**

An Offer in Compromise is a cash payment to the IRS for less than the full amount of the taxes owed in order to settle the liability. Although historically the IRS had been reluctant to accept most Offers in Compromise, an increasing number of IRS District Offices are now receptive to these plans as quick and practical methods of clearing up tax debts.

## IRS Criteria for a Payment Plan or Offer in Compromise

In general, a business with tax problems must meet some basic criteria in order to be considered for a payment plan or an Offer in Compromise, including:

- The business should not be a "repeater or chronic delinquent" i.e., a business with recurring tax problems.
- The business should have the financial capacity to catch up on its back taxes while at the same time staying current on future payroll tax obligations.

---

### Survival Tip #52

**The verbal or written testimony of experts can be helpful to a business that is trying to work out an installment plan or Offer in Compromise.**

---

The IRS will review the financial statements and past tax payment history of your business to determine if you meet their basic criteria. If you do, the agency's preference will be for you to clear up your debt through an installment plan since this option guarantees the IRS the most money. If an installment plan is not feasible, the agency may consider an Offer in Compromise.

If after reviewing relevant documents the IRS decides that you do not meet the criteria that it has established for an installment plan or an Offer in Compromise, it will give you an opportunity to pay your tax debt in full. If you can't, the agency will initiate enforced collection actions against you as explained in Chapter 7. If enforced collection is a possibility and you are not already working with a reputable bankruptcy attorney, find one immediately.

## Professional Help

Many business owners are not comfortable working with the IRS to arrange an installment plan or an Offer in Compromise and feel that they could get a better deal from the agency if they hire a professional to help them. This is a good idea for most small businesses since IRS rules and regulations are numerous, confusing and constantly changing. Also, it can be intimidating to try and hold your own with a revenue officer who is talking in IRS Speak. A professional who has experience working with the IRS will be familiar with the agency's processes and procedures and should be able to use this knowledge to your best advantage.

## Survival Tip #53

**There is evidence that the terms of an installment plan or an Offer in Compromise are directly proportional to the quality of the reputation of the professional who assists you in your discussions with the IRS.**

Tax or bankruptcy attorneys and accountants are professionals who can help you with the IRS. Be sure that the professional you hire has experience working with the agency on payroll tax problems. Also, before hiring a professional, it is important that both of you address how you will be kept apprised of the progress of discussions with the IRS. Insist on receiving proof from the professionals that any money you give them as full or partial payment on your tax liability actually goes to the IRS. In addition, ask the IRS to give you a receipt for the payment.

Good accountants are worth their weight in gold. They can help you deal with your IRS tax problems and can sometimes save you lots of money. However, a bad accountant can bury a business.

## *Know Your Accountant*

*Restaurant owner Fred W. had hired an accountant to help him resolve his business's payroll tax problems. Fred did not feel comfortable dealing with the IRS himself and wanted the accountant to intercede for him.*

*At first, everything seemed to be going fine. Even when the accountant told Fred that he had to come up with half of the $30,000 he owed the IRS if he wanted the agency to agree to an installment payment plan, Fred did not balk. Instead, Fred borrowed the money from his brother and turned it over to his accountant, assuming the accountant would in turn pay the*

*IRS. Not until months later did Fred discover that the accountant had kept the money and that Fred still owed the IRS $30,000!*

*Despite Fred's dilemma, I was convinced that he could avoid bankruptcy through an Offer in Compromise. Therefore, I referred Fred to an excellent accountant. Reluctantly, Fred scheduled an appointment, and eventually an Offer In Compromise was arranged.*

*I suppose this story has two morals. First, exhaust all options before considering bankruptcy. Second, if you decide to hire professionals to help you with the IRS, be sure that they have impeccable credentials and are totally trustworthy. Although Fred's situation is an example of extreme fraud, there are many professionals who make big promises and are unable to deliver on them.*

# The Form 433

If you want to resolve your tax debt through an installment plan or an Offer in Compromise, you must complete an IRS Form 433A, Collections *Information Statement for Individuals*, if you are a sole proprietor, or a Form 433B, *Collections Information Statement for Businesses*, if your business is a partnership or corporation. If you want to negotiate an Offer in Compromise, you'll also have to complete a Form 656, *Offer in Compromise*. (See Appendix B for sample forms.)

The four-page Form 433 is very similar to a bank loan application. The IRS will use this form to evaluate your financial condition and to help determine a reasonable installment plan or Offer in Compromise.

## Survival Tip #54

**Do not overestimate the value of the assets you list on your Form 433. It is better to err on the conservative side. Also, be sure that you accurately list *all* your expenses and not overstate your revenues.**

When completing a Form 433A, you will note on the third page that you must list and value your assets. If you own a car, use its *Blue*

*Book* value. The *Blue Book* is available at most public libraries and car dealerships.

If you have a home, a private real estate appraisal is generally the best way to determine its value. However, in some communities, a home's value for tax purposes may be appropriate for the Form 433. Therefore, before paying for a private appraisal, talk with a real estate agent to find out how closely private appraisals and tax appraisals compare in your community.

In order to avoid inflating the worth of your household assets, value them at what they would bring at a garage or estate sale. This method of valuation will be acceptable to most revenue officers.

---

### Survival Tip #55

**Provide your revenue officer with any documentation—utility bills, telephone bills, medical receipts, check stubs, etc.—that can substantiate the numbers on the paperwork you complete.**

---

If you are seeking an installment plan, you may be required to provide the revenue officer with 6 to 12 months of your most recent bank statements. These statements will be used to verify that your deposits are roughly equal to the revenues on your Form 433.

Ostensibly, the IRS uses Form 433 to help assess the viability of a business and to determine an acceptable installment plan or Offer in Compromise. However, the agency may also use the form to prepare for the possibility of enforced collection action in the future. If that becomes necessary, the IRS wants to be sure that it knows as much as possible about a business's assets.

## Working Out the Terms of an Installment Plan

To determine the terms of an installment plan agreement, a revenue officer will review your Form 433, comparing revenues to expenses. While doing so, the officer will make judgments regarding the necessity of your expenses. If the officer decides that a particular expense is unnecessary, the expense will be disallowed. In other words, the IRS will not include a questionable expense when calculating your business's total expenses. As a result, the amount of your regular payments to the IRS will be higher than if the expense were allowed. For example, if you are a sole proprietor and you are personally liable for both your personal and business debts, the revenue officer working on your case may not allow the cost of your child's private school tuition since you could send your child to public school and not incur that expense.

## Survival Tip #56

**Tell the IRS that you would like to make your installment payments on a weekly rather than monthly basis if your cash flow permits it. This will convey to the agency that you are serious about wiping out your debt, and it will make it easier for you to keep up with your payments.**

### The Terms of an Installment Agreement

If the IRS approves your installment plan, you will have two options: Accept the plan by signing Form 433D, which outlines the terms, or refuse it. (Refer back to Chapter 5 for an explanation of the appeals process.)

If you agree to the plan, your agreement with the IRS will run for an undefined period of time—as long as the IRS chooses—generally from one to five years.

All IRS installment agreements come with two very important conditions. First, throughout its duration, you must make all of your monthly installment payments in full and on time. Second, you must pay all future payroll tax dollars on time and in full. If you are late with a payment, miss a payment or are unable to meet future payroll tax obligations, you will be considered in default. When this happens, the IRS will initiate enforced collection actions, usually without any warning.

## Survival Tip #57

**If you are going to be late making a payment, if you cannot pay the full amount or can't make a payment at all, write _and_ call your revenue officer as soon as you know there is a problem and work with the officer to resolve it. Keep a copy of your letter.**

## Other Conditions

Depending upon circumstances, the revenue officer may impose additional conditions before approving your installment plan. For example, the IRS can demand that you:

- file and pay payroll taxes on a monthly rather than a quarterly basis;
- open a special bank account and deposit the appropriate amounts in the account within two days of paying wages to employees;
- promise in writing to get a paid job; or
- sell or mortgage certain assets and apply the funds to your tax liability.

---

## Survival Tip #58

**If you fail to set up a special account and make deposits in it as instructed, you may be found guilty of a misdemeanor.**

---

## Circumstances That Can Alter an Installment Plan

Assuming that you meet all of the conditions of your installment plan, it is unlikely that you will hear from the IRS while your plan is in effect. There are two exceptions—if your financial situation improves significantly or if the ten-year statute of limitation draws near.

Throughout the duration of your installment agreement, the IRS will monitor your financial situation so that any significant improvement is noted as soon as possible. If one is noted, you will be contacted about increasing the amount of your monthly payments.

---

## Survival Tip #59

**If the agency's computer shows that your financial situation has substantially worsened, it is unlikely that you will be contacted about lowering your monthly payments. *You* will have to initiate that change.**

If an installment agreement is still in effect as the ten-year statute of limitations approaches, the IRS will notify you that it intends to establish real and personal tax liens (the ten-year statute of limitations does not apply to liens) against your assets and that it will establish priority claims to those assets. The IRS will take this action to protect its interests because once the ten-year point has been reached, the agency can no longer continue to collect unpaid payroll taxes through an installment plan unless it has perfected liens against you.

### If an Installment Plan Is Not Approved

If the revenue officer refuses to approve an installment plan for your business, or if you find the terms of the plan unacceptable, you can appeal the decision of the IRS. However, it is also probably time for you to consider bankruptcy unless you can quickly come up with all the money you owe the agency. Otherwise, you can expect that the IRS will initiate enforced collection actions against your business.

## Conditions for an Offer in Compromise

You are a good candidate for an Offer in Compromise if you:

- are only one or two quarters behind on your payroll taxes;
- have no other tax problems;
- are in good financial condition; and
- are not a chronic tax abuser.

Your request for an Offer in Compromise must be based on one or both of the following conditions, and the IRS must agree that the condition(s) exists:

- You are financially unable to pay your delinquent payroll taxes in full.
- There is doubt as to your liability for the amount the IRS says you owe.

You must be able to provide evidence that supports the basis for your request for an Offer in Compromise.

If you base your offer on an "inability to pay," your offer must equal or exceed the current value of the equity in your assets plus your ability to make payments in the future. See Figure 6.1 for a worksheet to use when calculating how much to offer the IRS.

## Figure 6.1　Worksheet for Calculating an Offer in Compromise

### ESTIMATE OF OFFER AMOUNT WORKSHEET

1. List your assets and their current value.

| Home | _____ |
| Car #1 | _____ |
| Car #2 | _____ |
| Furniture | _____ |
| Boat | _____ |
| Other (list) | _____ |

2. List your liabilities.

| - Mortgage | _____ |
| - Car Note | _____ |
| - Car Note | _____ |
| - Loan Bal. | _____ |
| - Loan Bal. | _____ |
| - Loan Bal. | _____ |

3. Subtract COL #2 from COL #1.

= _____
= _____
= _____
= _____
= _____
= _____

4. Total amounts in COL #3. _____

**x .80**

5. Multiply the amount on line #4 by .80. _____

6. List other assets.

| Money in Bank | _____ |
| Accts., CD's, | _____ |
| Savings, etc. | _____ |
| Other Invest. | _____ |
| Other (list) | _____ |

7. List other liabilities only if secured by listed assets.

| - Other | _____ |
| - Other | _____ |
| - Other | _____ |
| - | _____ |
| - | _____ |

8. Subtract COL #7 from COL # 6.

= _____
= _____
= _____
= _____
= _____

9. Total amounts in COL #8. _____

10. Add amounts on line #5 and line #9.
**THIS IS YOUR TOTAL EQUITY VALUE.** _____

11. List your net monthly income, including amounts deducted for savings bonds or other savings allotments. (Both spouses' income if married) _____

12. Total your payments for rent or mortgage, utilities, vehicles, groceries, phone, gasoline, insurance, child care (if necessary for employment), and other necessary expenses. Do not include payments deducted from your paycheck. _____

13. Subtract line #12 from line #11. This is your monthly ability to pay. _____

**x 50**

14. Multiply the amount on line #13 by 50. **THIS IS THE CURRENT VALUE OF YOUR ABILITY TO MAKE MONTHLY PAYMENTS.** _____

15. Add the amounts on line #10 and line #14. This is your estimate of a potentially acceptable offer. All offers are subject to investigation and verification by the IRS. As a result, the final acceptable offer amount may differ from this estimate. _____

*If you have the ability to obtain the dollar amount on line #15, an offer in compromise may be the solution to your tax problem. Acceptance of an offer by the IRS requires that you file and pay on time all taxes due for the next 5 years.*

Pub SWR COL-33 (12-92)

If your offer is based on doubt, the degree of doubt will be a factor when the IRS evaluates your offer.

Your Form 656, Offer in Compromise, Form 433 and any additional documentation the IRS deems necessary will be reviewed to determine whether or not there is sufficient basis for an Offer in Compromise and the reasonableness of your offer. The agency will consider your net worth as well as the total amount of taxes you owe. Additionally, some consideration may be given to your age and health—the older and/or the less healthy you are, the more likely the IRS will accept a reasonable offer.

---

## Survival Tip #60

**The IRS will expect you to explore all possible sources of capital including bank loans, loans from family members or friends, an inheritance, etc. when making an offer.**

---

Generally, the IRS will not allow you to use an installment plan to satisfy an Offer in Compromise. However, short-term deferred payment offers with substantive initial payments may receive favorable consideration from the IRS.

---

## Survival Tip #61

**If the IRS rejects your offer, you'll be given an opportunity to improve it. You may also appeal.**

---

### Conditions of an Offer in Compromise

As a condition for granting an Offer in Compromise, the IRS may impose any or all of the conditions that were previously discussed in the section on installment plans. In addition, the agency can require that you agree in writing to pay it a percentage of future earnings or that you will relinquish certain present or potential tax benefits.

## Uncollectible Taxes

Occasionally, the IRS will categorize a business's tax liability as *currently uncollectible*. This means that the agency believes that neither an installment agreement nor an Offer in Compromise is feasible and that enforced collection actions are not likely to be productive.

When this happens, the IRS will monitor the future financial condition of the business through its tax returns. If a significant improvement is noted, the IRS will contact the business about clearing up its tax liability.

During the time that the taxes are categorized as uncollectible, penalties and interest will be accruing. In order to protect its interests, the IRS may also file a tax lien against the business's assets.

## Conclusion

Whenever you are unable to pay your taxes in full, your best option is to negotiate an installment plan with the IRS or work out an Offer in Compromise. When doing so, it is always helpful to get the assistance of an accountant or a tax or bankruptcy attorney who has experience dealing with the IRS on these matters. If neither of these options work out and you are unable to come up with a lump sum payment to the IRS, the agency will pursue one or more of the enforced collection activities discussed in the following chapter, and it is time to consider bankruptcy as a possible solution.

# IRS Collection Actions

*I*n this chapter, I will address the enforced collection actions that the IRS can take against a business that owes back taxes. I will describe how each action works and review what a business can do if the IRS moves against it.

## Collection Actions Available to the IRS

If you ignore all IRS correspondence about paying your tax liability or if you violate your payment agreement with the agency, you run the risk of the IRS taking an *enforced collection action* to collect its tax dollars. The specific action the IRS takes will be based on your circumstances and resources, as well as on the agency's analysis of your payment history and financial situation. The IRS will also take into consideration its understanding of general business trends and patterns in your industry.

Prior to pursuing enforced collection action, the IRS will give you several opportunities to voluntarily clear up your tax debt by mailing you a series of notices. Each notice will alert you to the fact that you owe money, ask you to pay up and warn you that it will take action to collect if the notices are ignored. The actions that the IRS may take include:

- filing a lien against one or more of your assets;
- serving a Notice of Intent to Levy;
- seizing and selling your property;
- closing down your business and liquidating its assets; and
- notifying those who are paying you interest and dividends to begin backup withholding.

## Survival Tip #62

**You can appeal the use of an enforced collection action.**

If you begin receiving notices from the IRS, you are in a very dangerous situation, and you have no time to waste! It is absolutely imperative that you do everything possible to avoid an enforced collection action. Such an action could signal the end of your business and the loss of valuable assets, damage your personal credit history and force you into bankruptcy. Seek the advice of a reputable bankruptcy attorney immediately; a reorganization bankruptcy is likely to be your only real option at this point.

## Survival Tip #63

**When enforced collection action is being threatened, it may still be possible to work out an installment plan or an Offer in Compromise. Seek help from a bankruptcy attorney who has experience dealing with such situations and who understands your options when your assets are being threatened.**

If you fail to respond to the IRS or you are unable to come up with the necessary dollars, the IRS will take one or more of the actions detailed on the following pages.

## The Tax Man Cometh

*Arnold J. called late one Thursday afternoon in a panic. At that very moment, an IRS agent was closing down Arnold's gasoline service station. Arnold had been working on paying off his back taxes but had gotten behind again. Now, on the busiest day of the week, the IRS was shutting him down.*

*After I finished speaking with Arnold, I asked to speak to the IRS agent in charge. As I suspected, the agent told me that Arnold's tax situation had deteriorated to the point that negotiation with the agency was no longer possible. Sadly, there was little I could do for Arnold that day.*

*The next day, I filed a bankruptcy and emergency motion for Arnold. Two days later, a judge ruled that Arnold could reopen his business if he agreed to resume making payments to the IRS.*

*Arnold was lucky. However, because he had become careless about his delinquent payroll taxes and was not demonstrating a good faith effort to work with the IRS, Arnold lost several days worth of much needed revenue and was forced into bankruptcy and costly legal expenses.*

## Filing a Lien

If the IRS files a lien against your assets, the lien will be for the total amount of your tax debt. In doing so, the IRS is publicly asserting that it has a claim against your property, including any assets you may acquire after the lien has been filed.

When a lien is filed, the IRS will also take steps to ensure that its claim against your property acquires priority status above all other creditor claims.

## Getting a Lien Released

To get a lien released, you must pay all your delinquent payroll taxes plus all applicable interest and penalties. You may also be able to get a lien released if you submit a bond to the IRS as a guarantee of payment. If the IRS agrees to a release, it will do so within 30 days.

## *Levies*

Levies are another type of enforced collection action available to the IRS. To satisfy a tax debt, the IRS may levy against your bank account, accounts receivables, contracts, etc., taking those funds or assets.

Generally, before the IRS can levy, three conditions must exist:

1. You must have received a *Notice and Demand* for payment from the IRS.
2. You must have neglected to respond to the notice.
3. You must have received a *Final Notice of Intent To Levy* from the IRS at least 30 days before it intends to levy.

However, if the IRS believes for some reason that the enforced collection of your taxes is in jeopardy, it can levy without observing all three conditions.

---

### Survival Tip #64

**When you fail to meet the terms of an installment plan or an Offer in Compromise, the IRS can levy against your accounts if it knows where you bank. Therefore, it is a good idea to open a second account after a payment arrangement has been finalized. Keep the majority of your funds in this second account, and use the first account to pay your taxes according to the terms of your arrangement. However, if the IRS asks you about your bank accounts after you have opened the second one, you must disclose the new account.**

---

If the IRS levies your bank account, your bank must hold any funds you have on deposit—up to the amount of the taxes owed—for 21 days. This gives you time to respond to the levy and to make payment arrangements.

At the end of the 21 days, if you have not taken steps to clear up your tax liability, the bank is required to debit your account for the full amount of your liability—or as much money as you have in your account—and to send the money to the IRS.

## Getting a Levy Released

The IRS is required to release a levy in the following situations:

- You pay the IRS the full amount of the taxes owed plus all applicable penalties and interest.
- The statute of limitations for the levy (the time during which the IRS can use the levy to collect) expires before the levy can be served.
- You and the IRS have worked out an installment plan or Offer in Compromise to clear up your tax debt. However, in some instances, the IRS will approve a payment arrangement but will not release the levy.
- The fair market value of the property being levied exceeds the levy, and the IRS believes that releasing part of the seized property will not jeopardize collection of the total taxes due.
- The IRS determines that the levy is creating an economic hardship.
- You are able to provide the IRS with evidence that releasing the levy will help it collect the tax.
- You file a Chapter 13 reorganization bankruptcy as a sole proprietor or a Chapter 11 reorganization bankruptcy as a business. Filing for bankruptcy will often get a tax levy released faster than going through normal IRS channels.

## Seizure and Sale

Another enforced collection action the IRS may take is the seizure and sale of your assets. Proceeds from the sale will be applied to your tax liability. Assets the IRS might seize include: vehicles, equipment and land.

---

## Survival Tip #65

**The agency will not pursue a seizure and sale if the estimated cost of those actions is more than the fair market value of the property it would seize.**

---

Prior to the sale of seized property, the IRS must provide public notice of the pending sale. In most cases, the notice will appear in the newspaper(s) of the county where the sale is to take place. Additionally, prior to the sale, the IRS must send you, via certified letter or personal delivery, the original notice of the sale. Generally, the sale will take place no earlier than ten days after you receive the notice; however, if the seized property is perishable, it can be sold right away.

---

## Survival Tip #66

**You have the right to request that your property be sold within 60 days. Typically, the IRS will grant this request unless it decides that it is in its best interest to retain the property.**

---

Prior to the sale, the IRS will establish a minimum bid price representing the lowest dollar amount it will accept for each item it is selling. This amount is usually at least 80 percent of the forced sale value of the seized property, less any liens.

In the event that you disagree with the minimum bid price, you may appeal by requesting that it be recomputed by an IRS valuation engineer or a private appraiser who can assist the IRS engineer. If you disagree with the second appraisal, you can obtain another.

Using the sale proceeds, the IRS will reimburse itself for the expenses of the levy and the sale. Remaining proceeds from the sale will be applied toward decreasing your tax liability.

If sale proceeds are not sufficient to pay the full amount of your tax liability, you will continue to owe the IRS, and interest and penalties will continue to accrue. If the sale generates excess funds, the IRS will provide you with instructions for requesting a refund. However, if a lien holder submits a claim superior to yours, the IRS will honor the superior claim first.

---

## Survival Tip #67

**Although filing a Chapter 11 or Chapter 13 bankruptcy will stop a seizure and sale and can force the IRS to return your property to you, liens will remain on the returned property until all your taxes have been paid.**

---

## Two Unwritten Rules of the IRS

While you will not find this written down in any of the information that you receive from the IRS, there are two types of personal assets that the IRS will usually not seize and sell. (Keep in mind that these unwritten rules do not necessarily apply to a business with a history of payroll tax problems.)

The first unwritten rule is that the IRS will not seize the home of a business owner or "responsible person." The agency does not like to kick people out of their homes and, in most cases, doing so is not financially advantageous for the IRS.

The decision regarding whether or not to seize a taxpayer's home is a business decision for the IRS—it must make economic sense for the agency. Therefore, to evaluate a possible seizure and sale, the IRS will consider a number of factors including:

- the cost of the seizure and sale;
- the cost of any necessary appraisals;
- the probable amount of money the house will sell for; and
- the amount of money the IRS expects to net.

### Survival Tip #68

**Seized property sold by the IRS does not usually go for market value.**

As a cushion, the IRS usually likes to assume an additional $10,000 worth of costs when calculating its return on the seizure and sale of a taxpayer's home.

### Survival Tip #69

**Although the IRS is reluctant to seize and sell a business owner's residence, if you have equity in your home, the IRS may demand that you refinance and give the proceeds to the agency.**

The second unwritten rule is that generally the IRS will not seize a business owner's individual retirement account (IRA) to help satisfy a tax liability. This is because the agency prefers not to take assets that are retirement-related.

### Getting Property Released Before It Is Sold

It may be possible to get seized property released prior to sale. This can happen if you:

- pay the amount of the government's interest in the property;
- enter into an escrow arrangement;
- furnish an acceptable bond;
- negotiate an acceptable plan for paying your back taxes;
- pay all taxes due plus applicable interest and penalties as well as the expenses of the seizure; or
- file a reorganization bankruptcy and motions for the judge to order the return of the property.

## Conclusion

The IRS is an extremely powerful federal agency as demonstrated by the measures that it can take to collect taxes it is owed. It is important that small business owners do whatever they can to avoid getting to the point that enforced collection action is even a possibility. However, if this does happen, it is important that a business owner recognize that he or she is in dire straits and that skilled legal advice is absolutely necessary. There is no time to waste at this point; all a business owner can hope to do is minimize the possible damage.

# Exit Strategies

*W*hen your business's problems are so serious that they cannot be resolved by pursuing the actions discussed in Chapter 4, or you decide that you no longer want to be in business, it is time to evaluate other strategies. Your options may involve closing down or selling your business, bringing in new management or filing for bankruptcy.

## Closing Your Doors

If you no longer want to be in business, you may be able to shut down without filing Chapter 7 bankruptcy. It is advisable to consult with both your attorney and your accountant before closing your doors. Get their input and advice about the best way to go about closing your business so that you do not unwittingly create future problems for yourself. If you are going to close your doors as a way of dealing with your financial problems, you will need to do the following:

- Hire an appraiser to value your assets so that you know what to ask for the assets you will liquidate. You should talk with your banker or accountant about this.

- Develop three plans—good, better, best—for paying off your creditors, and determine which creditors will get paid first. The *best plan* assumes that you get your initial asking price for most or all of your assets, which would provide you with the maximum amount of money to pay your creditors. The *better plan* assumes that you have to come down a bit from your initial asking price. The *good plan* assumes that you sell your assets for something less than what they would bring under the *better plan* scenario; the good plan would generate the least amount of money for your creditors.

- Contact your creditors, and attempt to negotiate debt pay-offs for less than you actually owe. Your creditors may be amenable to this because they will realize that you will not be filing bankruptcy, and they are assured of getting some money relatively quickly without the expense of collection or legal actions.

For a discussion of how to negotiate with your creditors, read the section in Chapter 4 entitled "Gaining Financial Concessions."

- Turn collateral over to your lienholders so the assets can be sold. Or, work out an arrangement with your lienholders to sell your collateral and provide the proceeds to secured creditors. Assets that you own outright that are not being used as collateral can also be sold and the proceeds used to wipe out debt. Talk with your banker about the best way of accomplishing a liquidation. Possibilities include: advertising in your local paper or in appropriate industry publications; using the services of a broker who will market your assets for a percentage of sales; contacting your competitors or other businesses that might be able to use your assets about their interest in purchasing them from you; using the services of a business auction house, etc.

- Use the proceeds together with any additional cash you may have on hand to pay off your creditors.

---

**Survival Tip #70**

**If you close your doors, you will have to give up your lease.**

---

## *The Graceful Exit*

*Alice B. came to me a year after she started her printing and copy business. Alice had given up a job as a successful salesperson with a major manufacturer of furniture to pursue the dream she had had since college, running her own business. However, things were not going well for Alice. She was paying all her bills but was not bringing anything home.*

*Alice and I looked at every possible way to cut costs and increase sales. No matter which path Alice took, however, her net income was simply not enough to provide her with anything more than a minimum wage. Alice needed to make more than that.*

*Alice and I talked about the best way for her to leave her business. We decided that Alice should approach her creditors with the possibility of working out deals that would allow her to pay a discounted amount to satisfy the balance she owed or to pay in installments that she could afford based on the income she anticipated once she found employment.*

*Alice was lucky; each of her creditors was willing to work with her given her good payment history with them. Alice closed her doors.*

*One of the reasons Alice was able to exit from her business with little or no harm to her credit history and no threat to her personal assets was that she had recognized early on that her business was not viable, sought professional advice and successfully pursued a decisive course of action. Closing her doors would have been far more difficult if Alice had waited until her business problems were serious, if she had defaulted on her debt or if she owed money to the IRS.*

## Selling Your Business

Another possible exit strategy is to sell your business. This is a viable option if:

- you are not in a financial crisis that necessitates bankruptcy;
- the tangible assets of your business would be of value to another business;
- with the right combination of management expertise and capital, your business could be viable; and
- your business's reputation has not yet been damaged by its financial problems.

How such a sale would be structured and the value of your business are both issues that should be discussed with your accountant, banker or a broker who specializes in the sale of businesses.

---

### Survival Tip #71

**If you decide to sell your business, be sure that you can support your business for the time that it will take to find a buyer. Otherwise, you may be forced into bankruptcy.**

---

## Ways To Sell Your Business

There are a number of ways to sell your business. The right method for you will depend on a variety of factors including:

- The location of prospective buyers
- Industry standards—Are businesses in your industry typically marketed in a certain way? Would deviation from that standard negatively affect the selling price of your business or how quickly it is likely to sell?
- The amount of time and money you have to spend marketing your business
- How quickly you need to sell your business

Consider the following methods of marketing your business to prospective buyers:

- Advertise in local newspapers, industry publications, etc. If you cannot afford a display ad, consider a classified ad.
- Contact your suppliers and your competitors to let them know that you are selling your business. Ask them to suggest potential buyers and to help you *put out the word*. One of your suppliers or competitors may be interested themselves.
- Ask your banker and accountant to suggest effective marketing vehicles and to refer potential buyers to you.
- Attend industry-related conferences, trade shows, etc. and network with attendees.
- Use the services of a broker. This is generally your best bet if you want to improve your chances of selling your business

quickly and for a good price, and if you don't have the interest or the time to handle the details involved in marketing your business and consummating a sale.

## Using a Broker

A business broker is a professional who helps business owners sell their businesses. The services of a broker can include the following:

- *Identifying every possible source of value in your business and helping you set a realistic asking price.* These values include features you might overlook that might be attractive to a potential buyer, such as your business's market share, its technology, real estate, equipment, inventory, as well as any tax losses your business may be expecting.

- *Helping you set a realistic asking price for your business.* An experienced broker will know how to price your business to ensure a quick sale. In determining a good asking price, a broker will probably not price your business assets at their full value. Therefore, before you accept the broker's suggested price, be sure you have a clear understanding of the rationale behind the price. Although you want to get as much money as possible out of the sale of your business, you want to avoid setting such a high price that it will not sell or will take a very long time to sell. Also, remember that any potential buyer is likely to do some hard negotiating to reduce your asking price. So, in setting a price, be very clear with the broker about what you need to net, and be sure that your asking price leaves you some negotiating room.

- *Developing and implementing a program to market your business.*

- *Locating qualified buyers.* A good broker can probably find a buyer for your business more quickly than you can because he or she is more apt to be aware of individuals and businesses in the market for your type of business. And, a broker will know how to screen interested parties to assure that they are truly qualified buyers.

- *Negotiating the terms of sale so that you are more likely to get the cash you need from the sale.*

- *Handling the paperwork and other details of the sale.*

There are a number of ways to locate a good broker—from talking to your banker or other creditors, to calling an industry association for referrals and talking to a reputable bankruptcy attorney or your accountant. Before hiring a broker, ask for the names of several financially troubled small businesses that he or she has recently sold, and ask each former business owner to comment on the broker's effectiveness and professionalism. Also, be sure that you are very clear about the terms of the agreement that a potential broker wants to have with you.

## The Broker Agreement

Prior to doing business with a broker, you and the broker will sign an agreement or contract that spells out the parameters of your relationship. Before signing, make sure you read the agreement carefully, and ask your attorney to review it.

It is usually a good idea to reserve the right to sell your business yourself without having to pay the broker a commission—usually about 10 percent for a small business. By doing so, you maximize the likelihood that your business will sell.

---

## Survival Tip #72

**When you are about to close on a sale—and not before—it doesn't hurt to attempt to get a broker to lower his or her commission. If your business is especially distressed, however, or if the broker is in hot demand, a commission concession is unlikely.**

---

Try not to tie yourself into an overly long agreement with a broker. That way, if the broker turns out to be ineffective, you can contract with another. Thirty to sixty days is a reasonable amount of time for an agreement, with an option to renew.

Before signing a broker agreement, be very clear about how the broker proposes to market your business. Plans should include advertising and a review of broker files for potential buyers.

## Preparing for a Sale

Talk with the broker you decide to use about any actions you should take that might expedite the sale of your business by enhancing its attractiveness to a potential buyer. Such actions might include:

- settling, consolidating or restructuring outstanding debts;
- organizing your financial records;
- making your retail space or offices as attractive as possible. (Consider a new coat of paint, getting your carpets cleaned, fixing a leaky roof, general housecleaning, etc.)

Do these things whether you use a broker or not.

## Bringing in New Management

A third alternative for dealing with a financially troubled business, if it has real potential for success and you want it to continue, is to bring in new management. Ideally, new management should contribute both capital and management expertise in exchange for partial ownership.

---

**Survival Tip #73**

**Avoid putting yourself in a situation where you give up management control but not ownership, since it is possible that the new manager could cause your business's situation to continue to deteriorate and you would be fully liable for the additional problems.**

---

Here are some ways to locate new management:

- Advertise in your local newspaper or industry publications.
- Contact professional associates.
- Contact your trade association.
- Talk to an executive search firm or headhunter that specializes in your industry and places people with management expertise.
- Talk with your banker and other professional advisors.

Before you begin your search, spend time thinking about exactly the sort of person you are looking for. Write the attributes you desire on a piece of paper. Include the management skills and experiences you are looking for, the amount of capital you'd like new management to bring to the business and the type of personality and business style you want in someone who will be managing your business. Involving new management in your business decisions can be stressful in the best of situations, but it can be disastrous if you and the new management do not share common values and attitudes or if your personalities are incompatible.

Develop a list of questions to ask the people you interview, and identify other types of information or documentation that would be helpful to your decision making. Be honest and open with potential new management about your business's financial situation and operations, its strengths and weaknesses, your goals for the business, your assessment of what it will take to achieve those goals, etc. Be sure to ask for references. When you do decide on new management, get your attorney to draw up a contract that clearly describes the terms of your agreement.

## Can Family Manage?

*Joe V. should not have been sitting in my office talking to me about his restaurant's business problems. At his age, he should have been retired and living off the fruits of his labor. In fact, Joe had retired 3 years ago after being in business for 30 years. At the time Joe retired, his business was quite successful. Things had changed.*

*Prior to retiring, Joe incorporated his business. Then, Joe invited his daughter's husband to continue operating the restaurant, telling him that if he did well, Joe would sell him the restaurant on reasonable terms. Joe fully expected that his business would continue to succeed under the management of his son-in-law. Joe moved to the beach and concentrated on fishing.*

*Three years later Joe's daughter was going through a difficult divorce, and Joe was back in town to help her through tough times. While there, he stopped by his restaurant, looking forward to seeing the faces of his old customers. When he walked into the restaurant, however, Joe discovered that his old customers had stopped coming, the restaurant's cash reserves were dangerously low and Joe's soon to be ex-son-in-law had not paid the business's payroll taxes for the three years he had been in charge.*

*As we talked, it became obvious that Joe had no way—short of closing his business—of paying his restaurant's back taxes. However, before he could close, Joe had to pay off the IRS. As a result, Joe came out of retirement to rescue the business his son-in-law had run into the ground. For Joe to protect his major personal asset —his home—he would have to run the restaurant long enough to pay off the IRS. And to do so, due to the condition of his business when he reinvolved himself with it, Joe was going to have to file Chapter 11 bankruptcy.*

# Bankruptcy

Bankruptcy can be an appropriate option for many financially troubled businesses depending on their financial condition, their chances for success if they get relief from their creditors and the actions that the IRS and other creditors may be threatening to take. The various types of bankruptcy will be discussed in detail in Chapters 9 through 12.

Bankruptcy is a good option under the following conditions:

- You owe back taxes to the IRS. You are unable to catch up or to negotiate an acceptable payment plan with the agency. You are afraid that the IRS will seize your business and/or personal property, levy your bank accounts or shut your business down.

- You are unable to pay your bills. You have not been successful at negotiating financial concessions with your creditors, bankers or suppliers and/or those concessions have not significantly helped your business. Your creditors and suppliers will no longer do business with you.

- Your secured creditors are threatening legal action to take back their collateral.

- Your landlord is threatening eviction and seizure of your property.

The most appropriate type of bankruptcy for you will depend on your particular circumstances and whether or not you want to remain in business. Read Chapter 9 to understand your options and the type of bankruptcy that is best for you.

## *Preparing for the Possibility of Bankruptcy*

This book has consistently emphasized the importance of consulting with a reputable, experienced bankruptcy attorney as soon as your business begins to experience financial problems. One of the purposes of early consultation is to obtain advice regarding the things that you can do to minimize the negative impact of bankruptcy on your personal finances and to help maximize the potential benefits of bankruptcy. Possible actions include transferring property into the name of someone else, under very limited circumstances, and changing your business's legal structure.

## Transferring Property

Many small business owners, even those whose businesses are incorporated, must sign a personal guarantee in order to obtain credit. This means that when a business's finances deteriorate, the personal assets of its owner, including vehicles, homes, furniture, etc. are at risk.

One way to deal with this problem is to legally transfer ownership of the assets you want to protect into the name of a spouse, family member or trusted friend. However, this transfer must be done at least one year before filing bankruptcy, or the bankruptcy judge can reverse the transfer and the assets involved will then be included in your bankruptcy. Therefore, it is extremely important before executing *any* property transfers to consult with an attorney. Property transfers that the court construes to be hindering creditors from taking your property and transfers done at the wrong time are illegal, although other transfers are acceptable.

---

## Survival Tip #74

**In a community property state, your spouse's guarantee is automatically guaranteed. Transfer into a spouse's name, therefore, will not offer your assets any protection.**

---

## Conclusion

If the actions already discussed in this book do not resolve your financial problems, then it is time to consider other actions, including shutting down, selling your business or filing for bankruptcy. The option that is best for you will depend on the financial condition of your business and whether or not you want to remain in business.

If bankruptcy is a serious option, be sure to meet with a bankruptcy attorney as soon as possible. This is important in order to ensure the success of your bankruptcy and to avoid actions that might jeopardize it. Chapter 9 provides an overview of your bankruptcy options, and more detailed discussion of each type of bankruptcy is provided in Chapters 10 through 12.

# Bankruptcy Options

*S*ometimes a business's best option is to file for bankruptcy. But, to use bankruptcy successfully, you must have a clear understanding about what bankruptcy can accomplish for your business. You must also select the most appropriate form of bankruptcy and complete as much prebankruptcy planning as possible.

A bankruptcy attorney can help you evaluate the best bankruptcy option for your business and can advise you on the actions that you must take prior to filing. If you are considering bankruptcy, however, you should have a general knowledge of your options prior to meeting with an attorney. Armed with information, you will be better able to understand and evaluate your attorney's advice and ask useful questions.

In this chapter, I will present an overview of the bankruptcy options available to various types of businesses. The three basic types of bankruptcy available to small businesses will be reviewed, as well as their pros, cons and limitations and a discussion of when each is appropriate. In addition, how a business's debts are categorized and treated in bankruptcy and what types of property certain types of business owners can keep will be reviewed. Selecting a bankruptcy attorney and the role and power of creditors in the bankruptcy process will also be addressed.

**Figure 9.1   When Is the Best Time To File for Bankruptcy?**

---

The following events should cause you to file for bankruptcy immediately:

- A creditor is about to win a judgment against you that will allow him to go after your business or personal assets.

- Taxing authorities like the IRS are threatening to shut you down because you are behind on your tax payments and have no way of paying them.

- Your business or personal real estate is about to be foreclosed on, and you want to stop the foreclosure.

- A creditor threatens to repossess your personal property, company equipment or vehicles.

---

## Prebankruptcy Planning

Planning for the possibility of bankruptcy, in consultation with an attorney whenever possible, should be done at the first signs of serious financial difficulty. It is unwise to wait until you are in a panic about your business problems and your judgment becomes clouded by the pressure of dealing with disgruntled creditors, customers and employees.

---

### Survival Tip #75

**Prebankruptcy planning is critical to the success of a Chapter 11 bankruptcy. Some attorneys suggest that prebankruptcy planning become a basic part of starting a business.**

---

Prebankruptcy planning gives you the opportunity to evaluate your options and select the best one. Such planning also helps you to realize the maximum benefits from bankruptcy. For example, the timing of a bankruptcy can affect its final outcome as outlined in Figure 9.1.

Many business owners ignore the early signs of financial difficulty and therefore don't seek advice about the best way to deal with their problems until their situation has deteriorated and they are in a panic mode. According to Sol Stein, "The sad fact is that in the vast majority of cases, a CEO hires a bankruptcy attorney after panic hits. He's been under the gun for some time. He is full of fear, anger and uncertainty, and he's fighting confusion and anxiety. That's not an optimum condition for making a wise decision. . . ."

There are a number of subjects that you should become familiar with during the prebankruptcy planning phase, including:

- property law and any exemptions that you may be entitled to if you are a sole proprietor;
- the rights of your creditors and how those rights may be exercised; and
- how your business's debts will be treated in bankruptcy.

Additionally, you should learn what actions not to undertake just prior to filing and which creditors should and shouldn't be paid before filing (see Figure 9.2).

If you plan to reorganize, use the prebankruptcy planning phase to ensure that all of your financial records are in order and that realistic operational and marketing plans are in place. These actions are especially important if you are planning a Chapter 11 bankruptcy since good business records and plans will help convince your creditors and the court that your business has the potential to complete a Chapter 11 and emerge as a viable entity.

---

### Survival Tip #76

**Avoid filing bankruptcy on an emergency basis whenever possible. Reorganizations that work best are those where the attorney and the business owner have sufficient time to develop tactics and to consult with other professionals.**

---

If you are contemplating Chapter 11, you should also use the prebankruptcy planning period to amass a *war chest*. You'll need this money to help pay your operating expenses during Chapter 11, as well as to pay fees for attorneys, accountants and other professionals and to negotiate deals with creditors before and during bankruptcy. A bankruptcy attorney should be able to advise you about the minimum amount of money to have in your war chest and possible sources of funds for this purpose.

**Figure 9.2   What Not To Do Prior To Filing**

Part of prebankruptcy planning involves finding out what actions might have a negative effect on your bankruptcy. Here are some basic rules of thumb for actions you should avoid taking if you are contemplating filing:

- Do not give preferential treatment to one or more creditor during the three months prior to filing, i.e., paying certain creditors to the exclusion of others. The payments can be voided by the court, and the money recovered.

- If you have loaned your business money, do not repay yourself immediately prior to bankruptcy. This action may be interpreted as preferential treatment.

- Do not give up anything that will limit your options once you file or give a creditor undue power over you.

- Do not transfer assets to friends or relatives in an effort to hide or protect an asset. You will be asked about this on the paperwork that you have to complete when you file.

- Do not run up your credit cards or obtain cash advances immediately before filing. If you do so, it is possible that the court will exclude that debt from your bankruptcy, and it will remain once your bankruptcy is over.

- Do not give creditors post-dated checks. If these checks bounce, you face criminal charges, and the bankruptcy will not protect you from any fines that may result or from going to jail.

**Survival Tip #77**

You can build a war chest by evaluating which creditors you'll need to do business with while you are in bankruptcy and which won't be needed. Keep up your payments to needed creditors and delay payment to others. Use the cash you would have paid your nonessential creditors to help build your war chest.

The prebankruptcy period should also be used to think through the likely responses of each of your secured creditors to your bankruptcy so that appropriate defensive strategies are identified and implemented.

---

## *Unconstructed*

*Darnell came to my office in a panic after scheduling an emergency appointment. The owner of a small construction company, he was typical of many small business owners that I see in my practice—Darnell had waited until his business was in crisis before seeking professional advice about the financial problems that resulted from his failure to pay payroll taxes.*

*It was Friday when Darnell came in. He told me that the IRS was threatening to close his business down the following Monday. In addition, Darnell told me that the agency knew he was nearly finished with a construction job and that they intended to take the money he would earn from it. Darnell said that if the IRS took those funds, he would be unable to pay his workers.*

*I told Darnell that his only option, given the seriousness of his situation, was to file a liquidation bankruptcy and shut down. I also explained that if Darnell had contacted me sooner, before his business was in a serious financial crisis, a Chapter 13 reorganization might have been a real possibility. Darnell could have bought himself time to get his business's finances in order while paying off his debt without fear of creditor collection actions.*

---

# Types of Debt

The federal bankruptcy code recognizes three basic types of debt—*secured, unsecured* and *priority*. Each is treated differently in bankruptcy.

## *Secured Debt*

Secured debt is the first type of debt to be paid in a bankruptcy. This is debt that a business has collateralized with an asset, and as a result, the business and the creditor essentially share ownership of that asset. For example, in order to obtain a bank loan, a manufacturing company may be required to give its bank a lien on a piece of its equipment or machinery.

Generally, a business cannot use bankruptcy to discharge or wipe out a secured debt without losing the collateral associated with that debt. This can be very problematic for a business that needs the collateral to operate. However, bankruptcy law says that to avoid losing a collateralized asset, a business may pay its creditor the value of the lien. That value is usually considered to be the worth of the collateralized asset at the time the bankruptcy was filed.

### Unsecured Debt

Unsecured debt is debt that is not collateralized. It is the last type of debt to be paid in a bankruptcy. This type of debt encompasses a wide variety of business liabilities, including:

- regular unsecured debt, such as credit card debt, trade credit, some small bank loans, loans from friends or family, etc.;
- criminal fines and certain court judgments; and
- child support and alimony.

Some unsecured debt is readily discharged through bankruptcy; some is not. For example, in most cases, child support and alimony are not dischargeable.

### Priority Debt

The definition of a priority debt depends on the type of bankruptcy. In a reorganization bankruptcy, priority debts are the ones that must be paid in full during the three to five years of the bankruptcy. Payment can be accomplished through monthly installment payments, a lump sum payment or some other arrangement. Priority debts include taxes and bankruptcy-related administrative expenses, such as attorney and accountant fees.

---

**Survival Tip #78**

**Some priority debts can only be discharged through Chapter 13.**

---

In a liquidation bankruptcy, priority debts get paid first. A business ranks its creditors in order of importance, and if there is money to be distributed in the bankruptcy, the creditor at the top of the business's list gets paid first, the second has second priority and so on.

## Exemptions

In any type of bankruptcy, the assets that belong to an individual who has a sole proprietorship are categorized as exempt or nonexempt. Exempt assets are considered to be essential or necessary to the business owner's ability to make a fresh start. Therefore, they will not be included in the owner's bankruptcy estate nor are they subject to seizure or sale by creditors or the court except by the lien holder. Partnerships and corporations are not entitled to exemptions.

---

**Survival Tip #79**

**Although an asset can be exempted from a bankruptcy, the lien on that asset may not be released. You may still have to pay the debt to keep the asset.**

---

Nonexempt assets are nonessential assets and therefore are usually included in a bankruptcy estate. All assets, whether exempt or not, must be listed in the debtor's schedules.

The federal bankruptcy code includes a list of the assets that an individual may claim as exempt. However, the code also says that individual states may develop their own list of exemptions. In some states, an individual may decide which set of exemptions to use. The exemptions to use should be decided with the assistance of a bankruptcy attorney and should be based on which are most advantageous to the business owner. See Figure 9.3 for a partial list of federal bankruptcy exemptions.

In a reorganization bankruptcy, business owners must indicate in their reorganization plans which assets they are claiming as exempt or nonexempt.

**Figure 9.3  Examples of Federal Bankruptcy Exemptions**

---

The federal bankruptcy code provides a list of exemptions available to the individual filing bankruptcy. The exemptions include (Bankruptcy Code Section 522 (d)):

- The debtor's aggregate interest, not to exceed $7,500 in value, in real property or personal property that the debtor or a dependent of the debtor uses as a residence, in a cooperative that owns property that the debtor or a dependent of the debtor uses as a residence, or in a burial plot for the debtor or a dependent of the debtor.

- The debtor's interest, not to exceed $1,200 in value, in one motor vehicle. A couple filing can each have a car with $1,200 equity.

- The debtor's interest, not to exceed $200 in value in any particular item or $4,000 in aggregate value, in household furnishings, household goods, wearing apparel, appliances, books, animals, crops or musical instruments that are held primarily for the personal, family or household use of the debtor or a dependent of the debtor.

- The debtor's aggregate interest, not to exceed $500 in value, in jewelry held primarily for the personal, family, or household use of the debtor or a dependent of the debtor.

---

If you file Chapter 7, you may be forced by your creditors or the bankruptcy trustee to give up all or some of your nonexempt assets or to liquidate them to help pay your debts. Your nonexempt assets can also be seized. However, Chapter 7 does allow business owners to keep nonexempt assets in the following situation:

- Business owners can purchase their nonexempt assets from the court-appointed trustee managing their bankruptcy case for a fair price.
- The trustee decides that a business asset has minimal liquidation value and abandons it rather than selling it. If this happens, the business owner can keep the abandoned asset.

If you file a reorganization bankruptcy, you may retain your nonexempt property as long as your unsecured creditors are paid at least the value of the nonexempt property in the reorganization plan approved by the court.

---

## Survival Tip #80

**Bankruptcy law values an asset at its market value—the amount it would bring on the open market if it were sold.**

---

Purchase money security agreements represent one important exception to exemption law. A purchase money security agreement is an agreement you sign when you borrow money to purchase an asset. Even if this asset is exempt, you must pay the creditor who financed the asset or risk losing it.

## Creditors' Rights

The federal bankruptcy code contains provisions that protect the interests of creditors affected by a business's bankruptcy and allows them to contest a business's decisions and actions during bankruptcy. Creditors can be especially powerful in a Chapter 11 bankruptcy where they can directly affect a business's efforts to reorganize and to make solid business decisions. In fact, it is not uncommon for hostile or especially aggressive creditors to become such obstructions that they force a business to convert to Chapter 7 and shut its doors.

---

## Survival Tip #81

**Creditors can complicate a bankruptcy by contesting the way their claims are categorized so that they can obtain a better position in the bankruptcy.**

---

Creditor inclusion in a business bankruptcy is not automatic. To have the opportunity to receive at least part of what they are owed by a business, each creditor must file a claim with the bankruptcy court after the business owner has filed bankruptcy.

## Creditors' Committees

In a Chapter 11 bankruptcy, the trustee may create a committee of unsecured creditors in order to give them an opportunity to wield more power as a group than they would as individuals. Such committees are rarely established in a small business Chapter 11 because generally these creditors are not owed enough money to justify the amount of time and money they will spend serving on such a committee.

There is never a creditors' committee in a Chapter 13.

## Options in Bankruptcy

There are three types of bankruptcy available to small businesses—Chapter 7, Chapter 13 and Chapter 11. Chapter 7 is a liquidation bankruptcy. Chapters 13 and 11 are reorganization bankruptcies. See Figure 9.4 for a comparison of these bankruptcies.

To decide the type of bankruptcy that is most appropriate for you, a number of factors should be considered, including:

- the legal structure of your business;
- the amount and type of your debt;
- the financial viability of your business; and
- your overall goal—to stay in business or to shut down.

To file any type of bankruptcy, you must complete certain paperwork and pay a filing fee. The filing fee for a Chapter 7 is $160; for a Chapter 13, $160; and for a Chapter 11, $800.

Once your bankruptcy has been filed, the court will issue an *automatic stay*, which prohibits your creditors from taking collection action against you while you are in bankruptcy.

Your bankruptcy will be a matter of public record and may affect your ability to operate your business efficiently and effectively. For example, after filing, you may have greater difficulty obtaining credit, and your suppliers may require that you pay cash up front for raw materials, office supplies, advertising space, etc. Bankruptcy may also affect your personal credit record—especially a problem if you are a sole proprietor.

**Figure 9.4  Comparison of Bankruptcies Available to Small Business Owners**

| *Type of Bankruptcy* | *Characteristics* |
|---|---|
| **Chapter 7 Liquidation** | • Available to all types of businesses who want to shut down.<br><br>• Filing fee: $160.<br><br>• Court-appointed trustee takes control of all assets (all the nonexempt assets of a sole proprietor), liquidates them and distributes funds to creditors.<br><br>• Most debts are wiped out.<br><br>• Process can take as little as five months. |
| **Chapter 13 Reorganization** | • Available to sole proprietors who do not owe more than $100,000 in unsecured debts and $350,000 in secured debts.<br><br>• Filing fee: $160.<br><br>• Reorganization plan must be approved by the court.<br><br>• Plan can exempt assets from the bankruptcy.<br><br>• Debt payments are made to a court-appointed trustee who disburses funds to creditors.<br><br>• Trustee does not control assets but receives and distributes business owner's payments to creditors.<br><br>• IRS cannot seize property while in Chapter 13, and debtor has up to five years to pay back taxes.<br><br>• Debts that remain after period of bankruptcy is over (three to five years) are wiped out. |

**Figure 9.4 Comparison of Bankruptcies Available to Small Business Owners (Continued)**

| | |
|---|---|
| **Chapter 11 Reorganization** | • Available to all types of businesses but generally not a good option for most small businesses. |
| | • Filing fee: $800. |
| | • Sole proprietors can claim exemptions. |
| | • Reorganization plan must be approved by the court and creditors. |
| | • Creditors can create obstacles to successful reorganization. |
| | • A creditors' committee may be formed. |
| | • There is no court-appointed trustee. Business acts as its own trustee, controlling its own operations; the U.S. trustee provides oversight only. |

## The Trustee

In Chapter 7 and Chapter 13 bankruptcies, the court appoints a private trustee—usually an attorney or an accountant—to be integrally involved.

In a Chapter 7 bankruptcy, the trustee takes possession of a business's assets and liquidates them to pay creditors after paying his or her own fees. In a Chapter 13 bankruptcy, the trustee recommends whether or not a reorganization plan should be approved, receives and distributes the business owner's payments to creditors and monitors compliance with the terms of the reorganization plan.

There is no court-appointed trustee in a Chapter 11 bankruptcy. As the *debtor in possession*, the business acts as its own trustee and manages its own operations without the trustee's interference. However, a U.S. trustee, who is an employee of the federal government, does monitor the business's compliance with the rules of the bankruptcy court to ensure that reorganization plans and monthly reports are filed on time and all necessary fees are paid.

### Chapter 7 Bankruptcy

A Chapter 7 bankruptcy is available to any type of business that wants to shut down or does not qualify for another form of bankruptcy. Typically, however, it is the choice of businesses with little or no hope of reorganizing.

The Chapter 7 process is relatively straightforward and swift. It can take as little as five months to complete. See Figure 9.5 for a description of who should file Chapter 7.

Once a business files a liquidation bankruptcy, it must immediately cease operating, and the trustee takes control of its assets. If the business is a sole proprietorship, all of its nonexempt assets become the property of the federal bankruptcy court. The trustee will liquidate all assets under his or her control either through sale or auction. The trustee will then deduct his or her fees from the proceeds and use the remaining funds to pay the business's creditors. This process will wipe out all but certain types of debt.

---

**Survival Tip #82**

**If you have a significant amount of tax debt in addition to other debt, consider filing Chapter 7 to wipe out as much unsecured debt as possible, and then file Chapter 13 to stretch out your payments to the IRS.**

---

## Reorganization Bankruptcies

Chapters 13 and 11 reorganization bankruptcies are generally used by financially troubled businesses that want to continue operating but need time to reorganize their debt and improve their operations free from creditor collection actions. Reorganization helps businesses get back on their feet by reducing their total debt and giving them an opportunity to repay remaining debt over a period of time through regular installments.

**Figure 9.5 Who Should File Chapter 7?**

Chapter 7 is a wise option if:

- a business no longer wants to stay in business or is no longer viable;

- a business has substantial unsecured debts that it cannot pay;

- a business does not have any substantial nondischargeable debts, such as federal taxes; or

- the business owner is a sole proprietor who is not interested in, cannot afford to keep or doesn't have nonexempt property.

## *Legal Structure Matters*

*Kathy N. started her employment agency after working as a temporary employee herself and recognizing that there was money to be made as a business owner. Through hard work and good contacts with personnel directors at several large companies in her area, Kathy was so successful that she began expanding her business. She began offering classes to train employees of local businesses, hired a bookkeeper to help her keep up with the financial management of her business, and on her attorney's advice Kathy incorporated her business.*

*Since Kathy was using temporary employees, she had a responsibility to send payroll tax money to the IRS. Kathy assumed that her bookkeeper was handling this. However, after her bookkeeper had been with her for some time, Kathy received an upsetting letter from the IRS. The letter said that Kathy's business was behind on its taxes and owed the agency $38,000.*

*Shortly after she received the letter, Kathy came to see me. She didn't know what to do since she did not have much money in savings and could not borrow $38,000. Therefore, Kathy wanted to know if bankruptcy would help.*

*After going over the pros and cons of bankruptcy, Kathy decided to file a reorganization bankruptcy. Because she had incorporated her business, however, Kathy was not eligible to file a Chapter 13, the best type of bankruptcy for her. To deal with this problem, Kathy decided to dissolve her corporation and then file Chapter 13.*

### Chapter 13 Bankruptcy

Chapter 13 is a court-supervised reorganization bankruptcy that lasts from three to five years. During a Chapter 13 bankruptcy, a business or individual makes monthly debt payments for most debts to the court-appointed trustee supervising the bankruptcy, not directly to the creditors involved. Some secured creditors, however, may be paid directly. If debt to unsecured creditors remains at the end of a bankruptcy, the court will erase the debt.

To be eligible to file Chapter 13, you:

- must be a sole proprietorship, and
- cannot owe more than $100,000 in unsecured debt or more than $350,000 in secured debt.

Chapter 13 is an especially important option for a sole proprietorship because the law does not distinguish between the personal and business assets of a sole proprietor. Therefore, if a sole proprietorship develops serious business problems, its creditors—including the IRS—can take legal action against the owner's personal assets. Chapter 13 allows a sole proprietor to protect personal assets while dealing with business troubles. Figure 9.6 outlines the types of situations appropriate for Chapter 13.

---

### Survival Tip #83

**Before filing Chapter 13, think about your suppliers. Will they still do business with you? Are there others who will? Will you be forced to go to an all-cash basis? If essential providers of goods and services won't work with you or will only do so on terms you can't accept, a reorganization bankruptcy may not be your best bet.**

---

If you file Chapter 13, you will have to prepare a reorganization plan and submit it to the court for approval. This plan will present your monthly income and essential expenses and will propose a debt payment schedule based on the dollars remaining after all your business's essential monthly expenses are paid. The plan will also indicate the exemptions you are claiming.

In a Chapter 13, it is not uncommon for unsecured creditors to receive only a fraction of the total amount they are owed. However, you will have to demonstrate in your reorganization plan that unsecured creditors will receive at least as much as they would if you had filed for Chapter 7.

**Figure 9.6    Who Should File Chapter 13?**

A sole proprietor or a husband and wife who own a business together should file Chapter 13 if:

- the individual or couple want to stay operating and the debt involved does not exceed the limitations for this type of bankruptcy;

- the individual or the couple who own a business together enjoy a steady stream of income;

- the individual or couple has a large number of priority debts or other types of debts that cannot be wiped out through Chapter 7;

- the business has a lot of nonexempt property that it wants to keep and enough cash to pay for the property; or

- the business is behind on payments for debt that it has collateralized and does not want to lose the collateral.

The goal of your reorganization plan should be to minimize the amount you have to pay to your creditors each month. The court, however, will want to be assured that the plan reflects the maximum amount you can pay each month. Therefore, if the court believes that you can pay more than your plan proposes, your plan will not be approved and you will have to develop a new one. Additionally, your plan will not be approved if the court does not believe that you have sufficient income to fund your reorganization plan. When court approval is not possible, your best option will be Chapter 7.

If you owe money to the IRS or to any other taxing authority, a Chapter 13 bankruptcy will not only protect your property from seizure, it will give you up to five years to pay delinquent taxes.

## Why You Reorganize

*Charles B. came to me when he received a letter from the Internal Revenue Service (IRS) threatening seizure of all his business assets. He was recommended to me by his accountant who could go no further in trying to resolve Charles's tax problems.*

*I reviewed Charles's situation, trying to determine if he had exhausted all nonbankruptcy remedies. Besides tax debt, Charles was deeply in debt to a bank and to a number of his suppliers. It quickly became obvious that Charles would have to file some type of bankruptcy.*

*As we began talking about bankruptcy, it was clear that Charles wanted to reorganize his business and had not given any thought to closing it. Charles was like most small business owners who don't like to think about ending their business because it makes them feel like failures. Sometimes, however, closing a business is the only thing to do.*

*Charles and I discussed Chapter 13 and Chapter 11 bankruptcy. We tried to determine whether his business would be profitable after a reorganization and whether he would be able to earn a good living from it.*

*Fortunately, because a reorganization bankruptcy would lower his regular debt payments, stretch out payments to the IRS, lower the total amount of debt he would have to pay and prohibit all his creditors from pursuing collection actions against him, Charles believed he could turn his business around and make a good living. Charles also believed that he had learned from his mistakes and that he would not get into financial trouble again.*

*Charles chose to use Chapter 13 bankruptcy to reorganize. But, to arrive at that decision, Charles had to understand exactly what his options were and the advantages and disadvantages of each. He also had to know what he wanted to accomplish through bankruptcy.*

## Chapter 11 Bankruptcy

Chapter 11 bankruptcy is available to all types of businesses. However, because more debt and a greater number of creditors are usually involved in a Chapter 11 than in a Chapter 13, the Chapter 11 process tends to be complex, time-consuming and expensive. Therefore, Chapter 11 is generally not a good option for most small businesses.

Chapter 11 works best for the business with enough resources that the staff time and the costs associated with it do not hinder the business's ability to function effectively day-to-day. Although good prebankruptcy planning can help improve a business's chances for success, it is estimated that as few as ten percent of all businesses that file Chapter 11 ever complete it. Instead, after months and even years of paperwork, hassle and expense, most businesses convert to Chapter 7. Figure 9.7 summarizes situations appropriate for Chapter 11 bankruptcy.

Sol Stein sounds an ominous note of caution when discussing Chapter 11. "Success in a Chapter 11 means getting out alive, and you've got 1 chance in 20. What you are doing in Chapter 11 is playing Russian roulette. If a businessman realized the odds against him, he would do everything in the world to stay out of Chapter 11."

The primary reason why success in Chapter 11 is so difficult is the power that federal bankruptcy law gives a business's creditors in this type of bankruptcy. Given the amount of money usually at stake and the inherent conflict between a creditor's desire to be paid as much as possible as soon as possible and a business's desire to keep its monthly payments as low as possible, creditors in this type of bankruptcy often take full advantage of their power in order to thwart a business's efforts to reorganize. When conflicts arise, the court will hold a hearing.

---

## Survival Tip #84

**A good attorney can help a business develop strategies for winning over troublesome creditors in a Chapter 11.**

---

As with a Chapter 13, the cornerstone of a Chapter 11 bankruptcy is the reorganization plan. This plan must be filed within 120 days of the bankruptcy filing.

In a Chapter 11 bankruptcy, a business's reorganization plan must be approved by its creditors as well as by the court. Approval from creditors can be a major stumbling block if relations between the business and its creditors are badly strained. Delay in approval will cause a business's legal expenses to mount and the energies and attention of its top management to become focused on getting the plan accepted, rather than on running the business.

### Creditor Conflicts

If you file Chapter 11, there are a number of issues around which you can expect creditor conflicts to arise, such as:

- the terms of your business's reorganization plan, including how you've categorized your creditors' claims, the amount of money your creditors will receive and the timing of your payments;
- whether or not you can use a collateralized asset prior to plan approval;

**Figure 9.7   Who Should File Chapter 11?**

A business should consider filing for Chapter 11 bankruptcy if:

- it does not qualify for a Chapter 13 bankruptcy, wants to continue operating and has an excellent chance of becoming financially viable if it gets relief from its debts;

- it has done prebankruptcy planning;

- it has an adequate amount of unencumbered funds set aside in a war chest;

- it has a strong management team in place;

- it has rational, non-hostile creditors willing to work with one another and with the business throughout the bankruptcy; and

- it has located an experienced, knowledgeable attorney with strong negotiating skills willing to represent the business.

---

- your bankruptcy-related administrative expenses; and
- your use of cash collateral.

For a detailed discussion of these issues, refer to Chapter 12.

## Legal Help

The ongoing involvement of an attorney is not always necessary in the simplest bankruptcies. However, as mentioned earlier, it is a good idea to consult an attorney for prebankruptcy advice. Consultation with an attorney is always advisable if you are in imminent danger of losing an asset, if your finances are complicated, if you are not good at managing paperwork and deadlines, if you are intimidated by the legal system or if you want to file Chapter 11.

### Selecting an Attorney

When selecting a bankruptcy attorney, try to find one who specializes in bankruptcy law, who has considerable experience dealing with the specific type of bankruptcy you are considering and who is familiar with your particular industry.

## Survival Tip #85

**In some states, attorneys can be board-certified to practice bankruptcy law. This means that they have passed a special examination, have practiced bankruptcy law for a number of years and have handled a substantial number of bankruptcy cases.**

There are many ways to locate a good attorney, including:

- *Referrals from trusted business associates who have filed and were satisfied with the attorney they hired.*
- *Referrals from other attorneys.*
- *A referral from your accountant.*
- *The bankruptcy court in your area.* Call this office, and ask if they can provide you with the names of some good attorneys. Although they are not supposed to refer you to anyone in particular, you may be able to find a clerk willing to tell you the ones who practice regularly in their court.
- *Listings in the Yellow Pages of your local phone book.* Look for bankruptcy lawyers under the heading *bankruptcy*.
- *Lawyer advertisements.* Although price is not the sole criterion to be used when selecting an attorney, lawyers who advertise often price their services very competitively. A lawyer who both advertises and specializes in bankruptcy law may represent an attractive combination.
- *Legal referral services.* Many cities and towns have lawyer referral services that you can use to get the names of attorneys. Sometimes these are operated by a city or county or state bar association.

## Survival Tip #86

**Do not ask for attorney recommendations from anyone with whom you are currently doing business. You will alert the business to what you are planning and possibly derail your plans or make them more difficult to achieve.**

If you are currently working with a law firm and are pleased with their services, don't assume that they should handle your bankruptcy even if they have bankruptcy attorneys on staff. Evaluate their bankruptcy attorneys as carefully as any other attorneys you are considering.

After getting names and telephone numbers, call the attorneys you are considering and schedule initial consultations. Be clear when you do so that you are in the process of shopping for an attorney, and ask if you will be charged for the first meeting.

At these meetings, explain your situation as well as the type of legal help you would like from an attorney. Do you want an attorney to take the entire case and be available to answer questions or to handle only a particular aspect of your case?

Find out how long the attorney has been practicing law, how much the attorney knows about your industry and how many bankruptcy cases he or she has handled personally for businesses similar to yours. You are not interested in how many such cases the attorney's firm has handled. Ask each attorney what type of bankruptcy they would recommend, and ask them all to identify potential problems or stumbling blocks in your case.

---

**Survival Tip #87**

**If an attorney you are considering suggests that your business file Chapter 11, get at least one additional opinion. There are unscrupulous lawyers who will recommend that option—not because it is in your best interest—but because they stand to make a lot more money than if you filed Chapter 13 or 7.**

---

Ask each attorney to outline fees and payment schedule. (If you are considering Chapter 11, try to find a lawyer who does not require a large fee up front and a big cash retainer.) If your bankruptcy is going to go on for at least several months, let the attorney know that you will expect to receive a monthly statement summarizing what has been done for you during the previous 30 days. Such a reporting requirement will help ensure that your money is being well spent. Figure 9.7 shows typical fee structures for each type of bankruptcy.

**Figure 9.7   How an Attorney Gets Paid in a Bankruptcy**

When and how the attorney will be paid depends on the type of bankruptcy.

- *Chapter 7.*   Attorney will generally expect to receive a substantial down payment on anticipated fees. This money usually comes from a business's pre-petition earnings or assets.

- *Chapter 13.*   Attorney can be paid from the approved reorganization plan.

- *Chapter 11.*   Attorney can demand a substantial up-front fee prior to filing, as well as a monthly retainer.

## Survival Tip #88

**Your attorney's legal staff may handle some aspects of your case. This will save you money since the staff's time will be billed at a lower rate than your attorney's.**

Evaluate an attorney on the basis of reputation, price, comprehension of your problems and ability to express clear solutions. Also, ask yourself if the attorney is someone you can trust and feel comfortable with. If an attorney seems overly busy or brusque, fails to answer your questions in a manner you can understand or acts condescending, look for someone else.

If you are going to file Chapter 11, there are some additional criteria you should consider during your attorney selection process. These include:

- *Negotiating skills.*   An attorney's ability to negotiate with your creditors can be critical to the success of your bankruptcy.

- *Ability to think quickly.*   An attorney handling a Chapter 11 case should be able to think clearly in the courtroom, even when faced with angry creditors and a difficult judge.

Joe Martinec, a Texas-based attorney who has handled a lot of Chapter 11 bankruptcies also suggests that a business consider the personality of an attorney. Joe says that an attorney's ability to read people and to know when to be charming or aggressive can be critical to the success of a Chapter 11, regardless of an attorney's credentials. Although personality traits may be difficult to assess, one way to do so is to observe an attorney in action in the courtroom.

After considering all the selection criteria spelled out in this chapter, hire the best bankruptcy attorney you can afford.

---

## Survival Tip #89

**Sometimes, a judge's decisions will be influenced more by the important clients handled by a law firm or by the frequency with which an attorney appears in his court, than by the merits of an attorney's argument. Unfortunately, the "more persuasive" attorneys are often priced beyond the reach of most small businesses.**

---

## Conclusion

Whether or not to pursue bankruptcy and the type of bankruptcy to file are serious and important business decisions that are best made in consultation with a good bankruptcy attorney. This chapter has provided advice regarding how to locate a good attorney and what to expect from the attorney. It has also provided an overview of the types of bankruptcy to consider and the bankruptcy process, emphasizing that if you want to reorganize rather than liquidate, your best bet, assuming that you meet the criteria, is Chapter 13, not Chapter 11. Chapter 11 is an expensive and time-consuming option and all too often, the business that files Chapter 11 ultimately converts to Chapter 7.

If you've decided, after reading this chapter that bankruptcy is your best option, it is time to read one or more of the next chapters to gain a more complete understanding of the type of bankruptcy you should choose.

# 10

# How Chapter 7 Works

*I*n this chapter, I will provide an overview of the Chapter 7 bankruptcy process with a focus on the sole proprietorship since that is the most common type of legal structure for a small business. However, when appropriate, I will also cover issues in Chapter 7 that relate to partnerships and corporations and will highlight the differences between Chapter 7 bankruptcy for sole proprietors and for partnerships and corporations. I will also discuss the role of the trustee and creditors in this type of bankruptcy and how sole proprietors can keep certain assets they don't want to lose through Chapter 7.

## The Chapter 7 Bankruptcy Process

Figure 10.1 summarizes events in a Chapter 7 bankruptcy. In a Chapter 7, all of a business's nonexempt assets and all assets that are not used as loan collateral are liquidated by a court-appointed trustee through sale or public auction. The resulting money is used to pay the trustee's fees. Then, based on the priority of the claims, the trustee will distribute any remaining funds among a business's creditors. Refer back to Chapter 9 for a discussion of the priority of claims in a Chapter 7 bankruptcy.

## Survival Tip #90

**In most liquidation bankruptcies, only a small fraction of creditors will actually get paid.**

Chapter 7 business bankruptcies fall into two categories—those filed by a sole proprietor, or individual, and those filed by a business, e.g., a partnership or a corporation. As discussed earlier, if you run your business as a sole proprietorship, you are personally liable for all your business's debts. Therefore, when your business fails and you decide to close it down by filing Chapter 7 to obtain relief from debt, you will actually be filing a personal bankruptcy.

## Survival Tip #91

**As you prepare to file for bankruptcy, do not let your secured creditors know what you are planning. If you do, you risk having them repossess your collateral before you've filed and have court protection from such action.**

When you file a Chapter 7 bankruptcy as a sole proprietor, you'll have to deal with such issues as exemptions, reaffirmation of debt and redemption of property and whether or not any of your debts are nondischargeable. None of these issues applies to a partnership or a corporation.

## Survival Tip #92

**It is possible for a sole proprietorship to continue operating after bankruptcy if the owner can exempt from the bankruptcy the assets he uses in his business. Talk with your attorney if this is something you want to consider.**

When a corporation or partnership files for Chapter 7 bankruptcy, it will stop operating the moment its case is filed with the court because all its assets now belong to the trustee.

**Figure 10.1  Events in a Chapter 7 Bankruptcy**

In general, events in a Chapter 7 bankruptcy will follow the sequence below. Every bankruptcy is different, however, so your bankruptcy may not follow this chronology exactly.

- Your bankruptcy is filed. All schedules of assets and debts should be filed at this time and exemptions claimed.

- The automatic stay goes into effect as soon as your bankruptcy petition has been filed, preventing further creditor collection activities.

- Your attorney should immediately notify your creditors of your bankruptcy. Later, the court will notify them too.

- The court will appoint a trustee to administer your bankruptcy case once it has been filed with the court.

- A creditors' meeting will be held 30 to 40 days after your bankruptcy has been filed. Your creditors and the trustee will have 30 days from the date of this meeting to object to any exemptions you may have claimed, and 60 days from the date of this meeting to object to the discharge of all of a sole proprietors' debt or to the discharge of a particular debt.

- The creditors listed on your schedule of debts can file claims against you from the time you file up until 90 days after the creditors' meeting.

- As soon as the trustee receives your bankruptcy case, he or she will begin determining which assets can be liquidated.

- All available assets will be liquidated and the proceeds distributed among your creditors after paying the trustee's fees.

- As a sole proprietor, your debts will be discharged by the court about four to six months after your case begins. If your business is a corporation or a partnership, you will not receive a discharge of debt. Instead, your case will be closed, which is the equivalent of a discharge.

- The trustee will conduct a final accounting of your case once all available assets are liquidated, or after it has been determined that there is nothing to liquidate.

- The court closes your bankruptcy case.

**Survival Tip #93**

> If your business is incorporated and you plan to file Chapter 7, do not pay yourself for any loans you may have made to it immediately before filing. If you do, the trustee will view the payments as preferential and may ask that you return the money. However, you can legitimately pay yourself a reasonable salary before closing your business down.

## *Difficult Decisions*

*It was a familiar reaction. Nancy and Patrick G. could not believe that they were not making a profit in their small grocery business. After all, so much money went through their hands every day! But, when I reviewed with them their income and expense statements for the past six months, it was obvious that they had not earned a profit. The money Nancy and Patrick were taking home to cover their personal expenses did not come from profits but rather from inventory that was sold and was not being replaced.*

*I asked the couple some questions about their business's finances. Their answers made me suggest that they close their business down, a suggestion that Nancy and Patrick had not anticipated. They told me they wanted to think about it.*

*On their second visit to my offices, Nancy and Patrick said they had thought about my recommendation and now realized that it was inevitable that they would have to shut down. We then turned to a discussion of how this might be accomplished. Since Nancy and Patrick's credit had been ruined and because they did not have any personal property that could be taken by the court, I suggested that the couple file a Chapter 7 liquidation bankruptcy. Once again Nancy and Patrick were surprised. They wanted to see if they couldn't work out something with their creditors. I responded that I did not believe that Nancy and Patrick would have enough money to satisfy their creditors. However, they decided that they wanted to try, and Nancy and Patrick left my office.*

*Six months later, after a lawsuit had been filed against them by a creditor, Nancy and Patrick finally decided that Chapter 7 was their best option. Like many other business owners, Nancy and Patrick resisted facing up to the inevitable and by delaying bankruptcy they further complicated their lives. As difficult as it may be, a liquidation bankruptcy is often a business owner's best solution to serious financial problems.*

## Schedules of Debts and Assets

To file a Chapter 7 bankruptcy, you will have to prepare schedules of your debts and assets as well as a statement of affairs. This should be done with the help of your attorney.

## Survival Tip #94

**If you have any money in the bank, be sure prior to filing that you take care of attorney's fees and that you pay as much as possible on your debt to the IRS. Also, make sure that the owners of your business are paid a reasonable salary.**

The schedule of debts is a list of all your debts including the dates they were incurred. These dates are important because if a debt is incurred close to the date you file for bankruptcy, the court may not allow it to be discharged. This holds true for some charges and cash advances as well.

When developing your list of debts, make it as complete as possible so that the maximum number will be discharged by your bankruptcy. Only those included on your schedule can be discharged.

Don't limit yourself to just the obvious creditors—those from whom you have borrowed money or from whom you've purchased something on credit. Think also of ex-partners, old customers and anyone with whom you have had a past business relationship. If there is a chance that people might come forward in the future and say they lost money as a result of doing business with you, list them as creditors.

## Survival Tip #95

**You cannot add creditors to your case once you have received your discharge.**

Before submitting your schedule of debts to the courts, review it carefully. Make certain that it is complete, that all applicable dates are provided and that all creditor addresses are accurate. If there are errors relating to the address of certain creditors, those debts will *not* be discharged because a creditor must receive notice of your bankruptcy for a debt to be discharged. Also, check to make sure that your descriptions of your collateral are complete and accurate and that your collateral reflects its fair market value— what you would get if you were to sell your collateral today.

## Survival Tip #96

**If the value of your property may be questioned by the trustee, go to the property tax office in your area and obtain an appraisal of your property. This document will help convince the trustee of your property's value.**

Your schedule of assets should be a complete and accurately described list of all your assets. When preparing this schedule, do not overestimate the value of your assets. This is because the more equity you have in your assets, the greater the likelihood that you will use up all your exemptions, and you'll be forced to give an asset to the trustee. For a discussion of exemptions, refer back to Chapter 9.

## Survival Tip #97

**When preparing your schedule of assets, do not overlook any claims you have against others. If you do not list a claim, pursue it and win, you risk losing the proceeds to the trustee. The trustee may also object to the discharge of your debts contending that you concealed the claim from the court.**

## Completing the Statement of Affairs

The statement of affairs is a series of questions that you must answer to ensure the court that you are being totally honest about your financial transactions and assets and that you are not trying to protect assets by giving them away as gifts or transferring them into the names of friends or family. You are prohibited from doing this within one year prior to filing.

---

## Survival Tip #98

**The trustee will view with great suspicion any transfer of property to family members. Therefore, be sure to discuss any such transfers with your attorney before filing.**

---

Be totally honest when completing the statement of affairs. If the trustee determines that you have tried to conceal certain assets so that you will not lose them, he or she will take steps to recover the assets and you may be liable for criminal penalties. Also, if the trustee determines that you have given preferential treatment to a particular creditor by paying that creditor at the expense of others, the trustee may make the creditor return the money. The trustee will then distribute the funds more equitably among all your creditors. You may also run the risk that the court will not grant you a discharge of your debts.

---

## Survival Tip #99

**If you think that any of your responses or actions may be viewed with suspicion by the trustee, talk openly with your attorney before filing your statement of affairs.**

---

# Delinquent Taxes and Chapter 7

In most cases, a Chapter 7 bankruptcy will not wipe out any of the taxes you may owe. Therefore, when your bankruptcy is completed, your tax debt will remain. However, while you are in bankruptcy, taxing authorities will be prohibited from trying to collect from you.

Under some circumstances, federal taxes can be discharged through a Chapter 7 bankruptcy. For example, if you are delinquent on income taxes and those taxes were due more than three years before you filed your bankruptcy, if you filed your income tax forms on time and the taxes were assessed more than six months before the filing of the bankruptcy, and if the IRS did not take a lien on your property, you may be able to get those taxes wiped out. Therefore, if you owe taxes, be sure to ask your attorney if they can be discharged. Remember, this discharge applies only to individuals; when a corporation or partnership owes taxes, the business's owners may find that the tax debt becomes their personal debt.

## The Automatic Stay and Creditor Notification

Once your schedules of debts and assets and your statement of affairs have been prepared and filed with the court, the court will invoke an automatic stay, stopping all creditor collection activities including actions by the IRS.

After an automatic stay is invoked, the court will notify all your creditors that they must immediately cease their collection activities. However, it is important for you to know that frequently there is a lag time between the point that the automatic stay is invoked and the point at which the court actually notifies your creditors about the stay. Therefore, rather than waiting for the court to take action, make sure your attorney notifies your creditors about the automatic stay and what it means. At a minimum, your attorney should contact all your secured creditors as well as any other creditors who have been especially aggressive in their collection activities.

If you don't want to use an attorney for the notification process, you can handle it yourself. It is less important who does it than that it gets done as soon as possible so that your creditors will cease their collection activity.

---

**Survival Tip #100**

**To make certain that your creditors are informed about the automatic stay, it is advisable to notify them via both phone and letter.**

---

The automatic stay applies to nearly all types of collection proceedings. For example, the stay will stop most lawsuits and, even if a creditor has won a judgment against you, the stay will stop enforcement of that judgment. Once the automatic stay is invoked, your home and other property cannot be foreclosed on nor can the IRS garnish your wages to get payment for back taxes.

## What an Automatic Stay Does Not Do

Despite its power, there are some things that the automatic stay cannot stop, including: criminal action taken against you and certain actions by the IRS. For example, despite an automatic stay, the IRS has the right to audit your company and to obtain information from you regarding a possible tax deficiency; however, the IRS cannot collect any money you might owe.

Theoretically, the automatic stay will stop an ex-spouse from collecting alimony, child support or maintenance payments from you. However, if at all possible, you should continue to make these payments because your legal obligation to pay child support, alimony, etc. will remain after your Chapter 7 bankruptcy is over. If you stop making the payments, most judges will issue a relief from the automatic stay to allow your former spouse to resume collecting them.

## Special Conditions of the Automatic Stay

If you are a sole proprietor in a Chapter 7, it is important to know that unpaid utility bills and unexpired leases can present special problems despite an automatic stay. For example, if you owe a large sum of money to a utility company, that debt will be wiped out through bankruptcy and according to the law the company cannot "alter, refuse or discontinue" service to you.

Within 20 days of the date that you file, there is nothing stopping the utility company from demanding a "reasonable" deposit if you have not already paid one. Generally, the court defines reasonable as an amount equal to two months of average service. Therefore, although the automatic stay will prevent disconnection of your service, to continue the service you may be required to come up with a substantial sum of money, something that may be difficult given your financial situation.

An unexpired lease presents another obstacle for the sole proprietorship in Chapter 7 bankruptcy. Although the automatic stay will stop a landlord from evicting you from your office, its effect lasts only until you decide whether or not you want to continue with the lease as it is written. Leaving your current space for a more affordable location will not present a problem. However, if you wish to stay where you are, you will have to become current on your lease payments. Depending on where you live, the time you have for becoming current could range from just a few days to a number of months.

---

**Survival Tip #101**

**If you are closing your business and are delinquent on an unexpired lease, be sure to remove all business records and personal property from the leased space before you file bankruptcy. Otherwise, you may find it difficult to get your property from your landlord later.**

---

## The Role of the Trustee in a Chapter 7

In a Chapter 7 bankruptcy, a court-appointed trustee oversees the process as the legal owner of all nonexempt assets involved in the bankruptcy and all assets that are not being used as loan collateral. To carry out their responsibilities, trustees:

- determine what property can be liquidated and how best to do it;
- determine the value of the property to be liquidated;
- investigate your financial affairs to make sure that all your nonexempt assets are identified and are controlled by the court;
- ensure that your creditors not inflate their claims against you; and
- with the court's permission, hire outside professionals such as lawyers, accountants and appraisers to help them carry out their responsibilities.

# The Creditors' Meeting

A creditors' meeting will usually be scheduled 30 to 40 days after an automatic stay has been invoked. If you are a sole proprietor, you and your attorney must both be at this meeting. If your business is a corporation or partnership, the designated representative should be in attendance.

---

**Survival Tip #102**

**Do not wear jewelry at a creditors' meeting. You risk making the trustee and your creditors think you have more assets to liquidate.**

---

Not all your creditors will attend the creditors' meeting. However, those who do will come to ask questions or to monitor the proceedings. Your unsecured creditors, for example, may attend to determine how likely it is that they will receive any of the funds that may be distributed. The unsecured creditors may also want to ask you or your attorney questions regarding your financial statements to assure themselves that you are being honest about your finances. If a creditor finds proof that you have lied on a financial statement, he or she can file a complaint asking that a debt be made nondischargeable. And if the creditor prevails, that debt will remain after your bankruptcy.

At the meeting, the trustee will ask you questions about your business affairs. Questions that might be asked include:

- Have all your assets been listed on your schedules, including any claims that you may have against other parties?
- What was paid to your business's owners before filing?
- Did you pay any creditors just before filing?
- Did you transfer property to anyone during the year prior to your filing? Were any of these transfers made to relatives?
- What was the basis for the valuation of your assets?
- Where are your assets located?

Answer all the trustee's questions honestly and completely. Remember, if you do not cooperate fully with the trustee, you could jeopardize the discharge of your debts, and you could be liable for criminal penalties.

The trustee may also request that you provide certain business records, such as past bank statements and copies of prior years' income tax returns.

## Survival Tip #103

**The trustee gets paid a percentage of any money administered through the liquidation process. Therefore, the trustee has an incentive to identify as many assets to be liquidated as possible.**

Although your attorney should tell you what to expect at the creditors' meeting, it is a good idea, prior to your meeting, to sit in on the creditors' meeting for a business similar to yours. By hearing what the trustee asks during the meeting, you will have a better idea of what to expect when your time comes. Also, observing other creditors' meetings should help alleviate some of the anxiety you may feel about your own meeting.

## Survival Tip #104

**If you are confused or worried by anything you hear at another business's creditors' meeting, talk to your attorney.**

### *After the Creditors' Meeting*

If you are a sole proprietor, your creditors will have 60 days after the creditors' meeting to object to the discharge of all your debts through Chapter 7, or to the discharge of a particular debt. Therefore, none of your debts will be discharged until this milestone is reached.

## Survival Tip #105

**If you are a sole proprietor and there are debts that you would like to reaffirm, now is the time to do so, before the 60 days are up.**

# Creditor Actions

Your creditors can respond to your Chapter 7 bankruptcy in one of two ways. They can:

- file a motion to lift stay if they are secured and want their collateral; or
- file a proof of claim.

Your creditors can file a motion to lift stay anytime during your bankruptcy. They must file their claims no later than 90 days after the creditors' meeting.

## Motion To Lift Stay

Secured creditors in a Chapter 7 bankruptcy frequently file a motion to lift stay, especially if they have a substantial amount of money at stake. They will use this motion either to get their collateral back or to get you to resume making payments on it. However, for such motions to be successful, your creditors must prove that you have no equity in the collateral and cannot afford to pay for it.

Creditors know that these two conditions are often difficult to prove. But, getting their collateral back is often not the creditors' real intent. Instead, the real intent of your creditors' motion may be to force you to resume making regular payments on your collateral. Therefore, it is not uncommon for creditors to seek "adequate protection" after they've filed a motion to lift stay. If the court rules that you must provide your creditors with adequate protection, you will have to begin making monthly payments immediately to your creditors.

## Filing a Proof of Claim

Most unsecured creditors, as well as many secured creditors, will opt to file a proof of claim once you've filed Chapter 7. When creditors do this, they are accepting the fact that you have filed and are putting themselves in line for any funds that may be made available.

## Survival Tip #106

**In certain situations, you may want to file a proof of claim for a creditor if the creditor has not done so. For example, you may want to make sure that the IRS is paid first to ensure that no tax liability survives your bankruptcy.**

# Your Assets

If you are a sole proprietor, you will need to decide which assets you want to keep and how to do so. In addition, your attorney will need to let your secured creditors know what you plan to do with your assets. Your options are to:

- keep an asset and continue making payments on it;
- give up an asset; or
- redeem an asset for its current value.

## Survival Tip #107

**Owners of partnerships and corporations may negotiate with their creditors to buy assets that they want to retain.**

### *Keeping Assets*

If you are a sole proprietor, the law says you can claim certain assets by exempting them from your bankruptcy. The assets you can keep will depend on the property exemptions available to you in your state as well as on available federal exemptions. The court will accept the exemptions you claim unless a creditor or the trustee objects to them within 30 days of the creditors' meeting. Refer to Chapter 9 for a discussion of exemptions and examples of federal exemptions.

If you want to retain an asset and are not behind on your payments on that asset, continue making the payments according to the terms of your contract while you're in bankruptcy. If you are behind on payments, your attorney should contact your creditor to negotiate a payment plan that will allow you to become current.

Your creditors will be amenable to working with you; however, they are not obligated to cooperate.

---

## *Strategies around Assets*

*Linda K. came to see me about filing bankruptcy because her bakery business had closed. Linda had many business debts to pay and wanted to find out if filing Chapter 7 would get her out of the mess she was in.*

*Like many others who consider filing this type of bankruptcy, one of Linda's biggest concerns was whether or not she would lose any of her property. She also told me that she was considering a move to Maryland and wanted to know if she should file a bankruptcy there or in Texas where she was currently living.*

*I explained that Linda could exempt certain assets and keep them, but that she'd probably lose most nonexempt assets. Then, she and I reviewed her assets to determine which could be exempted from her bankruptcy.*

*Linda's property consisted of a home with some equity in it, and the usual clothing, furniture and jewelry most people have. In addition, Linda owned a 1983 Buick, and she had a claim against a construction company that had done a bad job of adding a room onto her home.*

*In comparing the exemptions between states, it was easy to see that Linda would benefit from staying in Texas because the state offered more generous exemptions to its residents than Maryland. I explained that Linda could stay in Texas until her bankruptcy was over and then sell her house and use the equity to establish herself in Maryland.*

*Linda had one more problem though—her lawsuit. It would not be exempt under Texas law, so the trustee could settle the claim, use the money to pay her creditors and Linda would get nothing.*

*I explained Linda's choices to her. She could file Chapter 7 and give the trustee her interest in the lawsuit; she could file Chapter 7 and try to buy her claim against the construction company from the trustee; or, she could gamble, not file Chapter 7 and wait for the outcome of her lawsuit. If Linda won the lawsuit, she could pay off her creditors using the proceeds. But if she lost, or if the lawsuit dragged on, Linda risked having her creditors take collection action against her.*

*Linda decided to file for Chapter 7 bankruptcy and to gamble that she would be able to buy her claim from the trustee. As it turned out, she was able to do so for $1,500.*

---

## Reaffirmation Agreements

It is likely that any creditors willing to let you keep an asset will want you to sign a reaffirmation agreement stating that you do not want the debt to be discharged through your Chapter 7 bankruptcy. If you sign such an agreement, you'll have to attend a hearing before a judge. During that hearing, the judge will make sure that your creditor is not coercing you into signing the agreement and that you understand that the agreement can be rescinded within 60 days of its signing.

Creditors like reaffirmation agreements because such agreements provide them with post-bankruptcy protection. For example, if after your bankruptcy has been completed, you are unable to keep up with payments on a debt that you've reaffirmed, your creditor can repossess its asset and sell it. If the asset sells for less than what you owe, you'll be required to make up the difference.

Obviously, it is always best if your creditor will allow you to keep an asset and continue to make payments on it without having to sign a reaffirmation agreement. That way, if at some point you can no longer continue to make your payments, the worst that can happen is that the creditor will take the asset back. However, your ability to negotiate such an arrangement will depend largely on the strength of the relationship between you and the creditor.

## Redeeming Property

If you are a sole proprietor, you may keep certain types of exempt property by redeeming it through cash payments. Exempt property eligible for redemption is property that is worth less than what you owe on it. If you can pay your creditor the full market value of an asset, the right of redemption allows you to keep it.

If you want to redeem an asset, your attorney should contact your creditor to negotiate an agreement regarding its value. If you are unable to agree on a fair value, your attorney can file a motion to redeem the property and a hearing will follow. It will be up to the judge to determine the asset's value.

Relatively few sole proprietors take advantage of the right of redemption because, given their financial problems, they are usually not able to raise the necessary cash. In addition, should a hearing be necessary, the business owner's attorney will charge an additional fee, something few small businesses can afford.

*Nonexempt Assets*

The list of assets you'd like to keep may include property that you've not claimed as exempt. If you can afford to offer a fair price, you may be able to buy this property back from the trustee. It is likely that the trustee will want to liquidate any nonexempt property that has some value over and above what you owe on it. If the trustee does not feel that the property can be sold on the open market for a higher price, the trustee will probably allow you to buy it back. Ask your attorney to negotiate the buy-back for you.

## The Discharge Hearing

If you are a sole proprietor, the court will mail you an order of discharge at the end of your bankruptcy—usually about four to six months after your creditor's meeting. The order of discharge means that your debts have been wiped out. It also signals the fact that the automatic stay has been lifted and that you are no longer under the court's protection.

Once you receive the order, make copies of it and keep them in a safe place. In the event that sometime in the future you are contacted by a creditor demanding payment on a prebankruptcy debt, copies of the order of discharge will provide proof that you have gone through a Chapter 7 bankruptcy and have had your debts discharged.

Each major credit reporting agency—TRW, Trans Union and Equifax—should receive a copy of your order of discharge together with a copy of the schedules listing your debts. It is a good idea, a month or so after you've contacted these credit reporting agencies, to request a copy of your credit record from each of them to make sure that each report shows that your debt has been discharged.

---

**Survival Tip #108**

**To learn how to add information to your credit report and how to request a copy of your credit report, read *The Credit Repair Kit*, by John Ventura (Dearborn Financial Publishing, 1993).**

---

If your business is a partnership or a corporation, there will be no discharge. Instead, after all available funds have been distributed to your creditors, your bankruptcy case will be closed.

## Conclusion

If you decide that your best option is to close your business through bankruptcy, you will be protected against creditor collection actions once you file, and a court-appointed trustee will take control of your business. The trustee will liquidate through sale or auction all of your nonexempt assets if you are a sole proprietor and, after paying his or her own fees, will distribute the remaining funds to the creditors included in your bankruptcy. With several exceptions, the debts that remain after all your funds have been distributed will be wiped out.

# 11

# How Chapter 13 Works

*A*s explained earlier, Chapter 13 bankruptcy is available primarily to sole proprietorships, not to corporations or most partnerships.

Chapter 13 reduces the amount of money you will owe your creditors; it provides time for you to pay your debts—over a three-year to five-year period—and allows you to protect your assets while you're in bankruptcy.

In this chapter, I will provide more detailed information about Chapter 13 bankruptcy and discuss reorganization plans, how debts are treated and the roles of the trustee and creditors. Figure 11.1 summarizes the Chapter 13 process.

## Filing for Chapter 13

If your business is a sole proprietorship, you are personally liable for all your business debts. Therefore, if you file Chapter 13, you are essentially filing a personal reorganization. To qualify for Chapter 13, your personal and business debts must amount to less than $100,000 in unsecured debt and less than $350,000 in secured debt. If you do not meet these criteria, believe that your business is worth saving and want to remain in business, you'll have to file Chapter 11.

As with other types of bankruptcy, once your attorney has filed your bankruptcy petition with the court, you will be in bankruptcy and the court will invoke an automatic stay so that your creditors' collection efforts are stopped. When filing your petition, your attorney should also provide the court with complete and accurate schedules of your debts and assets. However, it is permissible under emergency situations for your attorney to file only the minimum amount of information necessary to have the stay invoked and then within the next ten days, to file the necessary schedules.

The cost of filing is $160. If you cannot afford this, you can petition the court to allow you to pay the fee in installments. A business filing for Chapter 13 rarely asks for this, however, because if it can't come up with the filing fee, it is unlikely that it can reorganize successfully.

Once your paperwork has been filed, the court will notify all your creditors to immediately cease their collection activities against you. However, as the previous chapter indicated, there is often a lag time between the time an automatic stay is invoked and the court actually notifies your creditors. It is always advisable to have your attorney notify your creditors right away—by letter, and by telephone—especially if a creditor is about to repossess one of your assets.

Your attorney should also begin contacting your priority and secured creditors to address any potential problems they may have with your reorganization plan prior to the creditors' meeting. Doing so can help expedite the bankruptcy process. Your attorney will talk with your creditors about:

- what you owe them;
- the value of your collateral; and
- how much in arrears you are on substantial debts such as mortgages.

Thirty days after you've filed, you must begin making payments to the trustee.

**Figure 11.1  Events in a Chapter 13 Bankruptcy**

Most Chapter 13 bankruptcies follow a typical sequence of events, although the events in yours may vary slightly. The usual sequence is:

- Your attorney files a *Petition for Relief* together with completed schedules of assets and debts. Your reorganization plan may also be filed at this time but if it is not, it must be filed no later than 15 days after your petition has been filed.

- Thirty days after your reorganization plan has been filed, you must begin making payments to the trustee.

- Forty to fifty days after your petition has been filed, the creditors' meeting will take place.

- Your creditors will respond to your reorganization plan by accepting it, filing a motion to obtain their collateral or by filing an objection to the plan.

- A confirmation hearing before a judge is scheduled. At the hearing the judge will listen to objections and decide whether or not your plan can be confirmed.

- After your plan has been confirmed, the trustee will begin disbursing money to your creditors.

- Your plan may be modified if something significant happens to necessitate change after the confirmation.

- After completion of your reorganization plan, you will receive a discharge of any debts that are not paid in full.

## The Reorganization Plan

No later than 15 days after you file your Chapter 13 bankruptcy petition, you must provide the court with a debt reorganization plan. This plan will present the amount you propose paying your creditors each month—your debt payment schedule—based on your monthly income and expenses. You and your attorney should prepare your plan.

## Survival Tip #109

**Be sure to provide your attorney with complete and accurate information about all aspects of your finances so that a reorganization plan can be prepared that will work for you. It is essential that you make your payments to the trustee on time and in full.**

When developing your plan, you should have two basic goals:

- Keep your monthly payments to your creditors as small as possible.
- Retain all the assets that you want to keep.

There are a number of other things to consider as you prepare your plan. First, be certain that you are claiming the maximum number of exemptions allowable because the number you claim will directly affect the amount of money you will have to pay your unsecured creditors. For a discussion of exemptions, refer back to Chapter 9.

Second, bear in mind the general dollar amounts that the court in your district thinks are reasonable for each item in your budget. Although most bankruptcy courts believe that all a debtor's disposable income after expenses should go toward paying debts, your reorganization plan should reflect the particular philosophy of the court in your area. If the budget in your plan diverges significantly from the standards in your district, you may have difficulty getting your reorganization plan confirmed.

### Types of Plans

There are a number of ways that a reorganization plan can be structured depending on the district in which you file your bankruptcy. Regardless of how it is structured, however, a reorganization plan cannot extend beyond 60 months, the plan must include both your personal and your business debts and it must be reasonable. Some of the ways that a reorganization plan can be structured include:

- You pay the same amount each month for a period of 36 to 60 months. This is how most reorganization plans are structured.
- Your payments increase gradually, with the smallest payments in the plan's first years and the largest in its later years.

This is a good option if your business is not generating strong profits now, but you expect that will change in the near future.

- If your business experiences seasonal highs and lows, your plan might reflect these fluctuations with higher payments in the good months and lower payments in the slower months.
- If you have assets that you want to sell with the intention of using sale proceeds to pay off some of your debt, your reorganization plan could reflect any of the above payment structures with allowance for large payments in the future after a sale has been consummated.

## How Your Debts Will Be Treated

When developing your plan, your attorney will take into account the nature of your debts. In a Chapter 13 bankruptcy, debts are typically divided into three categories—priority, secured and unsecured. If there is good reason, you may also designate creditors who will receive special treatment. These might include debts that were incurred because a relative co-signed a note for you.

### Priority Claims

Since priority claims represent debts that must be paid in full during the duration of your reorganization plan, your attorney should deal with them first.

You can pay off priority claims either by selling an asset or making regular monthly payments large enough to wipe them out while you're in bankruptcy. Federal taxes are a common example of a priority claim as are sales and property taxes.

---

### Survival Tip #110

**Stay current on your taxes after filing Chapter 13 and your plan is approved. If you get behind on your taxes while your plan is in effect, the taxing authority can ask the court to dismiss your case, and you risk losing the court's protection.**

---

## Cleaned Out

*Only a few days earlier, Edwin T. had completed a Chapter 7 bankruptcy. Now, I was preparing to file another bankruptcy for him. This time it would be a Chapter 13 reorganization.*

*When Edwin first came to my office, he knew that he had to close down his dry cleaning business. He had a lot of debt, including a $20,000 payroll tax debt to the IRS. A Chapter 7 bankruptcy would wipe out all of Edwin's business debt except for the taxes.*

*Edwin and I talked about the various ways the IRS could collect from him after his bankruptcy was completed. Edwin was afraid the agency would levy his wages from the company he was now working for. He was also worried that the IRS would go after his home, which had a large equity.*

*We talked about the possibility of making payment arrangements with the IRS, but Edwin told me that he had once had a bad experience with an IRS revenue officer and as a result, lacked confidence that the agency would give him a payment plan he could afford.*

*That's when I suggested Edwin file Chapter 13 bankruptcy immediately after his Chapter 7 was completed. This would offer him the continued protection of the court and five years to pay the taxes he owed. For Edwin, this seemed the safest solution to his problem.*

## Secured Debts

Secured debts are those that have been collateralized with an asset, like real estate, inventory, equipment or accounts receivables. Secured debts are further divided into money you owe on the house you live in and other debts secured by other property.

You can deal with your secured debts in several ways. If you want to keep a secured asset, you can usually modify the rights of the creditor by paying only the value of the collateral you pledged to get the credit, plus some interest, rather than the full amount owed. If you do this, payments on the value of the collateral should be made over the life of your reorganization plan. This is usually the option a sole proprietor chooses in Chapter 13.

Another way to deal with your secured debts if you file Chapter 13 bankruptcy is to return the collateral to your creditor so that it can be sold. Should proceeds from the sale be insufficient to wipe out your debt, the amount you owe will be termed a deficiency and will become an unsecured rather than a secured debt and treated like any other unsecured debt.

---

## Survival Tip #111

**If you have several types of property collateralizing the same loan, you can pick and choose the property you want to retain or give up. This is especially important if you have dead inventory or equipment that you are not using.**

---

Your third option is to pay your creditor the full amount of the claim according to your original contract rather than going through the plan. The only time you may do this is when your collateral is worth more than the balance of your debt.

---

## *Buying Your Assets*

*Jim B. owned a small trucking firm. He owed money to several banks with liens on his trucks, was three months behind on his payments and was being threatened with repossession of his vehicles. Jim had decided to file for Chapter 13.*

*One of Jim's trucks was worth very little and would have cost a great deal to repair. In the reorganization plan I helped him develop, this truck would be returned to the creditor in satisfaction of Jim's debt.*

*The other three trucks were in fair condition. They were needed to keep the business going. Jim owed $75,000 on these vehicles for total monthly payments of $2,500.*

*I explained to Jim that the rule in Chapter 13 bankruptcy is that if you pay the value of your collateral plus interest over the term of your reorganization plan, you can keep your asset. In Jim's case, the value of his trucks was $30,000. Jim was allowed to pay that amount over the term of his plan, which reduced his payments to less than a $1,000 a month. This reduction in monthly payments allowed Jim B. to stay in business.*

## Home Mortgages

Home mortgages represent an important exception to the first option presented in the previous section. Although you can use Chapter 13 to save your home from foreclosure and to deal with delinquent home mortgage payments by paying them over the life of your organization plan, you cannot modify the rights of your mortgage holder. In other words, although you can pay off back mortgage payments through monthly installments, you must continue to make your regular house payments while in a Chapter 13.

---

### Survival Tip #112

**Usually you will be given three years to take care of delinquent home mortgage payments. However, if you need more time, your attorney can ask for up to five years.**

---

## Non-Purchase Money and Non-Possessory Secured Liens

Non-purchase money and non-possessory secured liens on household goods or *tools of the trade* present a sole proprietorship in Chapter 13 with a special opportunity. These liens exist when a finance company asks you to pledge your household goods or tools of the trade as collateral in order to borrow money. Since the money you borrowed was not used to purchase the property you pledged, those funds are considered nonpurchase money; and since you, not the finance company, have possession of the property, the funds are considered non-possessory. In many states, the law says that you may void the lien a finance company has on your household goods or tools of the trade and treat the company's claim as an unsecured claim.

## Unsecured Debts

After your attorney deals with your priority and secured debts, he or she must determine how much you can afford to pay each month on your unsecured debts. The minimum amount you pay your unsecured creditors will depend on how much nonexempt property you own.

It is with these debts that you can realize real benefits through Chapter 13, because the court can make substantial reductions in the amounts you have to pay your unsecured creditors. As long as your plan treats all your unsecured creditors the same, the court will usually allow you to pay them less than 100 percent of what you owe them. You can also realize significant savings, because, while you are in bankruptcy, you are usually not required to pay interest on your unsecured debts.

## Creditor Responses to Your Bankruptcy

Within 90 days of the first creditors' meeting, each of your creditors must file a proof of claim with the court so that the debt you owe them will be included in your bankruptcy. Secured creditors who fail to meet this deadline may forfeit the right to be treated as secured creditors and will receive less money under your plan.

Unsecured creditors who do not file a proof of claim by the deadline may forfeit the right to be treated as unsecured creditors and may receive no money at all.

Either before or at the creditors' meeting, one or more of your creditors may object to your plan. Generally, they will object because they do not like the way they are being treated in it. To object, creditors must file an Objection to Confirmation of the Debtor's Plan, explaining their objection.

If creditors file an objection, it is your attorney's responsibility to contact them to ensure that the objection is valid and to see if anything can be worked out without the court's intervention. If a compromise cannot be negotiated, a hearing will be held and the objecting creditor, possibly joined by an attorney and witnesses, will attend the hearing together with you and your attorney. Although your attorney will represent you, you may be asked to testify. A judge will listen to both sides and make a decision about the objection. If the judge decides in favor of your creditor, you will have to adjust your plan accordingly.

## The Role of the Trustee in a Chapter 13 Bankruptcy

After you file Chapter 13, a trustee will be assigned to your case. Prior to confirmation of your reorganization plan, the court-appointed trustee will investigate your financial affairs to help determine whether or not to recommend approval of your plan.

After confirmation, the trustee will receive your debt payments and distribute them to your creditors. The trustee will also monitor your compliance with the terms of your reorganization plan and may help you do so through advice and assistance. The exact amount of advice and assistance you receive will depend on your trustee. Some actively work with debtors and have even developed special programs to help them do a better job of managing their money. Others, however, will offer little or no advice.

---

### Survival Tip #113

**Unlike the trustee in a Chapter 7 bankruptcy, the trustee in a Chapter 13 will not take over and control all your assets since the goal of a Chapter 13 is to keep your business operating.**

---

The trustee will be paid out of the monies you pay your creditors. The bankruptcy code says that up to ten percent of what you pay your creditors can go to administrative expenses and to pay the trustee's salary. However, the actual percentage your trustee receives will depend on your district.

## The Creditors' Meeting

Forty to sixty days after your bankruptcy petition has been filed with the court, the creditors' meeting will take place. Generally, this is the first opportunity that you will have to meet the trustee assigned to your case. Your creditors may also attend the meeting and may bring their attorneys. Some creditors will attend out of curiosity. Others may use the meeting to object to your plan if your attorney was unable to work out their problems with your reorganization plan prior to this meeting.

---

### Survival Tip #114

**In order not to jeopardize your plan's chances for confirmation, inform your attorney *before* the creditors' meeting if there is any change in your financial situation or if you have forgotten to mention something that affects your situation.**

---

## Evaluating Your Plan

A trustee and judge will use six basic criteria to evaluate the reasonableness of your plan. It is your attorney's responsibility to ensure that your plan meets these criteria:

1. Your plan must comply with all the rules and provisions of Chapter 13. All the paperwork you are required to file should be complete and should adhere to the rules of your district as well as to bankruptcy procedures. In addition, all necessary papers should be filed on time.

2. Your plan should be proposed in *good faith*. This can be a stumbling block to approval for some debtors since what constitutes good faith varies from judge to judge. The most common example of *lack of good faith* is one that pays unsecured creditors very little or nothing.

3. Your unsecured creditors must receive at least as much as they would have received if you'd filed Chapter 7. To ensure this, some debtors opt to pay their creditors over a 60-month period, the maximum amount of time a Chapter 13 reorganization plan can be in effect.

4. You either give your collateral to your secured creditors, or you pay these creditors the value of the collateral plus interest during the duration of your plan. Your secured creditors also will retain the liens they have on your collateral. If you decide to keep your collateral by paying your creditors the value of the collateral, the court will make sure that you can afford to do so before confirming your plan.

5. You can make the payments set out by your plan. The court wants to be assured that you have the income to meet the terms of your plan and that your budget is realistic.

6. You are paying all your disposable income to your creditors.

## The Confirmation Hearing

At the confirmation hearing, the trustee will present your reorganization plan to a judge and recommend that it be approved or disapproved. Generally, this hearing is rather perfunctory, since in most cases the judge assumes that the trustee has reviewed the plan and therefore will accept the trustee's recommendation. Each district is different, however, so talk with your attorney before the hearing to find out what to expect. Also, find out if you have to appear at the hearing. If you do, dress neatly and conservatively.

## Conversions, Modifications and Moratoriums

Sometimes our best laid plans are thwarted by circumstances that we cannot anticipate. Therefore, if something unexpected happens and you cannot make your payments as spelled out in your reorganization plan, the bankruptcy system has safeguards to protect you. These safeguards include asking the court to allow you to skip making payments for a few months if a suspension of payments would help you regain control or modifying your entire reorganization plan to make it reflect your changed circumstances. Another option, if changed circumstances point to the need for closing your business rather than reorganizing it, is to convert from a Chapter 13 to a Chapter 7 bankruptcy.

## Discharge of Debts

Discharge of your debts will occur once you have completed your reorganization plan. This will take place somewhere between three and five years after your plan goes into effect. This time period will be shorter if some of your creditors do not file claims in your case and are not included in your reorganization plan.

---

**Survival Tip #115**

**If at the end of your plan you have not paid all your unsecured creditors, the bankruptcy code will discharge the debt that remains.**

---

## Conclusion

If you are a sole proprietor and want to remain in business but need relief from your creditors while you get your financial situation under control, Chapter 13 is usually your best option. Filing Chapter 13 will also reduce the total amount you owe your creditors.

After filing, you will prepare a reorganization plan detailing how you plan to pay off your debts as well as the assets you want to keep. After the court approves your plan, you'll make your payments to a court-appointed trustee who will also make sure that you are meeting the terms of your reorganization plan. Once you've completed your reorganization plan—usually after three to five years—your remaining debts will be discharged.

# How Chapter 11 Bankruptcy Works

*A*s explained earlier, Chapter 11 bankruptcy is usually neither a good nor a realistic option for a small business. This is due to the expense, time and complexity of the Chapter 11 process. However, in some situations, Chapter 11 is appropriate for small businesses. Therefore, in this chapter my intention is: to persuade businesses for which Chapter 11 is not appropriate to pursue other means of addressing their financial problems and to provide important and needed information to those businesses for which Chapter 11 is a viable option.

## Planning for Chapter 11

The earlier you begin planning for the possibility of Chapter 11 bankruptcy, the greater your chances for success. As stressed throughout this book, the importance of involving a qualified, experienced attorney in the prebankruptcy planning process is extremely important.

During prebankruptcy meetings, your attorney should provide you with an overview of the Chapter 11 process and help assess your chances for success. Figure 12.1 summarizes events of the

Chapter 11 process. If your lawyer does not consider your business to be a good candidate for Chapter 11, an alternative approach to your financial problems should be pursued.

Before making a final decision about Chapter 11, be sure to review the emotional considerations laid out in Chapter 2. Chapter 11, more than any type of bankruptcy, can place severe emotional strain on you and your family.

Assuming that you decide to go forward with Chapter 11, there are a number of subjects critical to the success of your bankruptcy that you and your attorney should talk about, including:

- *How much Chapter 11 is likely to cost and where the money will come from.* Most Chapter 11 attorneys will not take a case without a large retainer that could range from $2,500 to $25,000 for a small business.

- *Actions you should and shouldn't take prior to filing.*

- *How you plan to finance your business's operations once you've filed, since not having access to adequate cash can force a business in Chapter 11 to convert to Chapter 7.*

- *Which collateralized assets you need to keep operating and how you can keep them, as well as which you are willing to give back to your creditors.*

- *Your creditors—who they are, the nature and amount of your debt to them, which creditors are more likely than others to present problems, etc.*

- *Possible strategies to diffuse creditor objections to your bankruptcy.* These strategies include negotiating agreements with creditors for *adequate protection* to minimize the probability that the creditors will take defensive actions harmful to the success of your bankruptcy. The best time to negotiate these is after you've filed and have the court's protection.

- *Which creditors to continue paying and which creditors to stop paying.* Your goal should be to minimize any disruptions in your business's operations by keeping your relationships with key creditors as normal as possible.

- *How you will continue to manage the day-to-day affairs of your business once you have filed, knowing that most of your time may be taken up dealing with the details of the bankruptcy and with possible creditor conflicts.* According to Sol Stein, the small businessman who files Chapter 11 "is not going to be running his business; he will be running the Chapter 11 business."

**Survival Tip #116**

> **Despite your best efforts, it is likely that once you file bankruptcy, some of the creditors who have extended you trade credit in the past will continue to do business with you only on a COD basis. However, if you had established a pattern of slow payments, some of your creditors may have put you on cash-only terms even before you filed bankruptcy.**

During the prebankruptcy planning period, you and your attorney also should discuss the income tax ramifications of filing Chapter 11 to determine if there are financial transactions that should be completed after filing. You may need to consult with a tax accountant on this subject.

Possible *bar dates* should be addressed. A bar date is the date after which the court will not allow a creditor to file a proof of claim. Claims filed after that date will not be included in your bankruptcy. Typically, the court will set the bar date for 90 days after the creditors' meeting.

Other things that you should do prior to filing include:

- Ensure that all of your tax returns are filed if you're behind.
- Obtain an informal appraisal of all real property you've used as collateral.
- If you are incorporated, and even if your officers are relatives, make sure that your board's minutes reflect your decision to file for bankruptcy.
- Plan the changes you need to make in your business to help ensure that your business's reorganization will be successful and that your financial problems do not recur.

## *A Boom and a Bust*

*Mike F. had built up a small company that he'd inherited from his father. Mike's business, an electrical contracting firm with mostly commercial accounts, was incorporated, but Mike held 100 percent of the company's only outstanding stock.*

*Mike's business fortunes mirrored those of the real estate industry in his state—first a boom and then a bust. During the boom, as his business expanded, credit was readily available to Mike, and he got heavily in debt. And, when the bust arrived, Mike was not prepared for its impact on his business. As a result, Mike began struggling to pay his bills.*

*Mike came to me because he wanted to keep his business operating and therefore was interested in a Chapter 11 reorganization bankruptcy. However, Mike waited until his creditors were about to foreclose on his collateral to come to me. Instead of having enough time to plan for Chapter 11, Mike was forced to file immediately. Further hampering his potential for success in Chapter 11, the accounts receivables Mike was counting on to pay his operating expenses while in bankruptcy were tied up with a loan. And, the bankruptcy judge had required Mike to use part of those funds to provide adequate protection to the creditor.*

*In the end, Mike never had the cash flow he needed to make Chapter 11 work. Months after he had filed, and after an agonizing period of trying to make his business profitable, Mike was forced to convert to a Chapter 7 bankruptcy and to close his business.*

*Addressing serious financial problems early in their development may be the only way a small business can hope to succeed in Chapter 11. Although filing for bankruptcy will provide a business with temporary relief from its creditors, the business may be forced to battle its creditors again in court to get a reorganization plan approved and, after approval, to operate efficiently and effectively.*

## Once a Chapter 11 Is Filed

Once you file, just as in other bankruptcies, the automatic stay will go into effect, providing you with immediate relief from the collection actions of your creditors. Several weeks to a month later, you will receive a notice from the court that an initial meeting has been scheduled with your creditors. If you do not attend this meeting, your bankruptcy may be dismissed. If the original date is not good for you, the U.S. trustee will usually—for a valid reason—reset the date of your creditors' meeting.

At the first creditors' meeting, the trustee will question you about the schedules you included with your bankruptcy petition. You also will be questioned about your compliance with the various written instructions you received from the court immediately after filing.

This meeting can provide your creditors with an opportunity to gather information that they will use to determine how to respond to your bankruptcy, e.g., be cooperative, file motions, etc. During this meeting, you may come under stiff questioning from your creditors who may question some of your past business decisions, your current business operations, financing decisions you've made, the nature of a particular debt, and the financial viability of your business. If your relationship with your creditors is already strained, this meeting may become confrontational. However, remain calm and polite, and try not to act defensive.

---

## Survival Tip #117

**If your business relationships have not deteriorated badly, the creditors' meeting presents you with an opportunity to establish or reinforce in your creditors' minds the viability of your business. The meeting also presents you with an opportunity to lobby the creditors to cooperate with you in order to increase the likelihood that your efforts to reorganize will succeed.**

---

After you file, your creditors will begin filing claims to ensure that they are included in your bankruptcy. Your creditors can continue to do so until the bar date set by the court. You will have the right to object to any of your creditors' claims. Reasons for you to file an objection include:

- You disagree with the value of your collateral. This is especially important if you are *cramming down* a creditor. For information about cramming down, turn to the section of this chapter entitled "The Reorganization Plan Approval Process."
- You disagree with the amount of a creditor's claim.
- You disagree with the classification of a claim—secured or unsecured.

If you object to a claim filed by a creditor, the creditor must respond or the claim will automatically be denied. If the creditor responds, a hearing will be held to consider the contested claim. If the court disallows the claim, you will not be obligated to include it in your reorganization plan, or it will be included under conditions set by the court. Any claim that you do not object to or that the court allows must be included in your reorganization plan.

**Figure 12.1   Events in a Chapter 11 Bankruptcy**

---

Every Chapter 11 is different, so there is no way to specify the exact sequence of events in this type of bankruptcy. However, the sequence below reflects the way events commonly occur:

1. Prebankruptcy planning begins.

2. Your bankruptcy is filed, and the automatic stay goes into effect.

3. You seek the court's approval to use your cash collateral.

4. Your creditors are notified of your filing, and they can begin filing their claims.

5. The first meeting with your creditors is scheduled.

6. Your business begins preparing its disclosure statement and reorganization plan. After filing, you will have 120 days to prepare and file these statements with the court.

7. Your creditors can object to your business's reorganization plan and/or disclosure statement.

8. The court approves or disapproves your disclosure statement.

9. Your creditors vote on your business's reorganization plan.

10. The court confirms or denies the plan.

---

## The Trustee in Chapter 11

There is no court-appointed trustee in Chapter 11 bankruptcy except in unusual circumstances. You will manage your business as the *debtor in possession*. You will be expected to maximize the use of your assets to comply with all reporting requirements and to ensure that as many creditors as possible get paid. Once a reorganization plan has been approved, you will be expected to comply with its terms. After your case has been filed, the U.S. trustee (a government employee, not a court-appointed trustee) will monitor your business to make sure that you are complying with your responsibilities as the debtor in possession.

## The Creditors' Committee

As indicated in Chapter 9, a creditors' committee is not formed in most small business Chapter 11 bankruptcies. However, in the event that a creditors' committee is established, the U.S. trustee will appoint to it the unsecured creditors in your bankruptcy with the largest claims.

## Your Responsibilities after Filing

Many misguided business owners think that once they file for Chapter 11, their work is over and their attorney will take care of everything. In fact, your work will have just begun. Explains Harlingen, Texas bankruptcy attorney Abe Limon, "It is the responsibility of a debtor to turn his business around from day one."

Success in a Chapter 11 is very much a partnership between business owner and attorney; both must work hard to ensure success. One of your most important responsibilities will be to take decisive steps to address your business's problems so that they will not recur. Doing so is also important to gain the confidence of your creditors so that they will be more apt to support your reorganization plan.

Taking decisive action may not be easy since you may have to fire employees, cut salaries and reduce benefits. You may also have to sell unneeded equipment, liquidate less profitable areas of your business and introduce other cost-cutting measures.

## The Disclosure Statement

Immediately after filing, you and your attorney should begin preparing a disclosure statement for your business. This document must be submitted to the court no later than 120 days after you've filed.

Your disclosure statement will provide information about your business to help your creditors decide whether or not to approve the reorganization plan you propose. This statement must be submitted to the court before your reorganization plan is submitted. Typically, a disclosure statement includes:

- a statement of your business's financial condition and an explanation of why you are filing for Chapter 11;

- a rationale for the reorganization plan that you are proposing and a summary of the plan; and
- a history of your business and a description of the qualifications and experiences of its top management.

The court will hold a hearing on your disclosure statement. Be prepared for the possibility that certain creditors will object to information in your statement or lack of certain information. Their objections may cause the court to delay approval of your plan.

## The Reorganization Plan

During the first 120 days after filing, you will have the exclusive right to prepare your own reorganization plan. If you fail to meet this deadline, however, your creditors may develop reorganization plans for you and submit them to the court. Needless to say, a creditor-developed reorganization plan is probably not in your best interest. In fact, many creditor-developed plans amount to little more than the liquidation of a business.

---

### Survival Tip #118

**It is a good idea to begin work on your plan as early as possible, since it can be a time-consuming document to prepare and is strategically important.**

---

### Survival Tip #119

**A business can ask the court to extend the time during which it has the exclusive right to prepare a reorganization plan. However, extensions are rare except in very complex bankruptcies.**

---

If more than one plan is submitted to the court, each will be considered. The court will decide which is in the best interest of all creditors, including equity shareholders if your business is incorporated.

## Survival Tip #120

**Creditor developed reorganization plans have become increasingly popular.**

### *Preparing Your Reorganization Plan*

When developing your reorganization plan, deciding how to group your creditors' claims becomes a critically important decision. It is critical because your creditors will vote to approve or disapprove your reorganization plan on a class-by-class basis according to the way you have grouped your creditors in your plan. Therefore, creditors should be grouped in a manner that will increase the likelihood that each class will support your reorganization. Also, be sure that the classifications make financial sense for your business.

## Survival Tip #121

**Classification does not change the priority of your creditors' claims.**

The bankruptcy code gives you considerable flexibility in grouping creditor claims as long as you can provide a solid rationale for the groupings. However, your plan must treat all creditors within the same class the same way unless a creditor has agreed to less favorable treatment.

The bankruptcy code does require that certain types of claims be grouped together—administrative claims, priority tax claims and claims incurred during the period between the date you filed and the date the court approves your bankruptcy petition.

The bankruptcy code also requires that your reorganization plan do the following:

- Identify each class of claims as either *impaired* or *unimpaired*. (See discussion of these terms on the next page.)
- For each impaired class, indicate which creditor(s) will be paid, how much each creditor will be paid and the timing of the payments.

- Identify the creditors who will not be paid or who will be paid less than what they are owed.
- Provide specific details regarding the disposition of property and the cancellation or modification of liens.

Additionally, your reorganization plan must:
- Give all creditors at least the present value of what they would receive if your business were liquidated and the resulting cash distributed among them as per a Chapter 7 bankruptcy.
- Provide payment in full of all priority claims either through a lump sum payment or through installment payments over the life of your bankruptcy. Typically, these payments are made monthly, quarterly or annually. IRS taxes must be paid within five years.
- Provide for the cash payment in full of all post-filing administrative expenses at the time the plan is approved.
- Comply with all provisions of the bankruptcy code as they apply to Chapter 11.
- Be proposed in *good faith*.

---

### Survival Tip #122

**When possible, avoid having to make balloon payments to creditors in a specific class. These payments can be a significant financial burden for a business in Chapter 11.**

**In developing a reorganization plan, you and your attorney should discuss which collateralized property you want to keep and which you will give back to creditors, recognizing that liens on property survive bankruptcy. Remember, you can pay just the current value of the collateral you want to keep.**

---

## Impaired and Unimpaired Creditor Claims

Creditors with impaired claims in your reorganization plan will not receive the full amount of money they are owed or may not receive their money according to the terms of the agreement you had with them originally. Therefore, if you anticipate trouble getting your reorganization plan approved, you can expect these creditors to be the likely source of conflict.

Creditors with unimpaired claims, however, will receive all that they are owed according to the terms of your original agreement. These creditors include:

- creditors receiving the full cash value of their claim in your reorganization plan, and

- creditors whose legal, equitable and contractual rights are not altered by your plan.

Additionally, if your plan indicates that you will clear up all missed payments on a debt and resume making regular payments to a creditor per your original agreement, that creditor has an unimpaired claim in your bankruptcy.

---

## A Compromise Arrangement

*I could see how upset Frank C. was when he told the bankruptcy judge how much money he needed to keep his company operating on a day-to-day basis. It was clear to everyone present that to stay alive the business would need most of the money it was generating until Frank could institute changes that would make his business profitable enough to propose a payment plan to his creditors. Payday for Frank's employees was just two days away. If the judge ruled that Frank could not use his receivables, he'd be unable to pay his employees and would be forced out of business.*

*The bank with a lien on his receivables was not being cooperative. It did not trust that the changes Frank was proposing would succeed, so the bank wanted all of Frank's business's money to go toward reducing the debt he owed to them. However, the judge trusted Frank. As a result, the judge ordered a compromise arrangement that gave both Frank and the bank something, but not as much as either wanted. As a result, Frank was able to meet payroll but not much else.*

*In order for Frank to reorganize successfully through Chapter 11, all available money had to go to the business. There was no money for Frank's salary, no matter how small. Ultimately Frank's business succeeded, but he and his family paid a price for that success. Fortunately, they were a closeknit family and were able to weather the tough times.*

## Financing Your Business While in Chapter 11

After filing Chapter 11, financing your operations can become a serious problem. Potential sources of operating funds include your war chest, your cash collateral and new credit. For information on "war chests," refer back to Chapter 9.

---

**Survival Tip #123**

**Your war chest may be quickly depleted by the expenses of filing and working your way through the bankruptcy process, leaving little for your business's operations.**

---

### Cash Collateral

To obtain a line of credit or a loan, you probably pledged your accounts receivables, securities, rent income, cash, etc. to the bank extending you the credit. This is termed cash collateral.

As soon as your Chapter 11 bankruptcy has been filed, your attorney should attempt to negotiate agreements with your creditors regarding use of your cash collateral. If these agreements are not negotiated and a creditor objects to your use of the funds, a hearing will be scheduled, and while you're waiting for the court's decision, they'll be unavailable to you.

At the hearing, the court may decide that you can use your cash collateral *with no strings attached*; it may allow you to use your cash collateral if you pledge a different asset to the creditor; or the court may say it's okay to use the cash collateral if you make "adequate protection payments" to your creditor. The court may also deny your use of the cash collateral and, depending upon your financial situation, this decision may force you to liquidate rather than reorganize. You can also be forced into Chapter 7 if your cash collateral battles are costly and protracted and if you lack sufficient unencumbered funds to finance your operations while the issue of your cash collateral is finally resolved.

## Survival Tip #124

**If you have given a creditor a security interest in your accounts receivables and you need those funds to make payroll, be sure you time your filing for just after you pay your employees so that you have time to get permission to use those funds before the date of the next payroll.**

### New Credit

Another post-filing financing option is taking on new debt. However, this is a long-shot for the average small business, and if the additional credit is "outside the everyday course of business," you must get the court's approval before you apply for it.

To increase the likelihood that you can obtain additional financing, the bankruptcy code says that the creditor agreeing to the financing can have super priority status in your bankruptcy. This means that your debt to that creditor will assume a better status in your reorganization plan than any other creditor.

## Survival Tip #125

**Family members and friends may be your best bet for additional credit once you've filed.**

One possible source of new financing is a creditor who has already extended a significant amount of credit to your business. Your argument to this creditor should be that the additional funds will help strengthen your business and protect the original claim.

## Survival Tip #126

**There are lenders who specialize in extending credit to businesses in Chapter 11. Ask your banker or accountant for some names.**

## The Power of Creditors in Chapter 11

According to Sol Stein, "If creditors applied rationality to the situation, they would really be one team, not against the small business." However, conflicts with creditors can be very common while you are waiting for your reorganization plan to be approved because the bankruptcy code gives creditors a lot of power. For example, your creditors can prevent or delay approval of your reorganization plan; they can make it difficult for you to meet your business obligations and can impede your ability to make smart business decisions. Worst of all, creditors can force you into a liquidation bankruptcy if they create enough delays or generate enough expenses for your business while you are trying to prepare your reorganization plan and get it approved.

---

**Survival Tip #127**

**A good attorney can help you develop strategies for winning over troublesome creditors.**

---

Creditor conflicts are very common in Chapter 11, because your goals and those of your creditors are different and there is usually a lot of money at stake. In Chapter 11, your creditors will be concerned about protecting their claims and about receiving as much of what they are owed, as quickly as possible. Your business, however, will be fighting for its life. To survive, you will need to retain all your essential collateralized assets, keep your monthly payments as low as possible and spread out for as long as possible, and use your cash collateral to help finance day-to-day operations.

Frequently, creditors will retain attorneys to fight their battles for them, adding to the expense of Chapter 11. And when battles start, they will be resolved through court hearings, often creating long delays and additional expense for your business.

Here are some common sources of conflicts with creditors before confirmation of your reorganization plan:

- The information in your business's disclosure statement
- The terms of your reorganization plan
- Your use of collateralized assets and cash collateral
- The payment of administrative expenses related to your bankruptcy

Additionally, after your reorganization plan has been confirmed, creditor conflicts can focus on whether or not you are meeting the terms of your reorganization plan.

### Questioning the Disclosure Statement

Your creditors may dispute the accuracy of information in your disclosure statement. For example, they may contest your business's financial condition to build a case that you cannot reorganize successfully, or they may call into question the business management abilities of you or your key staff.

### Terms of the Reorganization Plan

Creditors may object to the way that their claim is categorized in your reorganization plan, the amount of money they will receive in your plan and the timing of your payments to them, among other things. Some creditors may even contest the very fact that you are reorganizing, reasoning that they will be in a better position if you file Chapter 7.

Responding to creditor objections to get your plan approved may necessitate the negotiation of side agreements with certain creditors. For example, you may have to make cash payments to certain creditors or make concessions to them, e.g., you may need to reclassify problem creditors so that they have a more advantageous position in your plan and will approve it.

## Use of Collateralized Assets and Cash Collateral

According to the bankruptcy code, between the time you file for Chapter 11 and the time your reorganization plan is confirmed, you may not make any payments on prebankruptcy unsecured debts.

Some of your secured creditors may file motions with the court to lift the automatic stay as it applies to their assets so they can repossess their collateral. The loss of important assets may seriously hinder your ability to run your business and reorganize successfully. Sometimes, the loss of a key asset can be tantamount to liquidation.

When a motion to lift stay is filed, you will have 30 days to respond or the automatic stay will automatically be lifted. If this happens to you, you can file an objection to the motion. If you do so, there will be a hearing, and the court will decide how to resolve the situation. Or, you can contact your creditor through your attorney in order to negotiate an acceptable payment arrangement so that you can use your collateral. The court must okay anything you and your creditor agree to do.

---

### Survival Tip #128

**If you decide to work directly with your creditor, protect yourself from the possibility that the negotiations may continue beyond the 30-day deadline for filing an answer to the motion by filing one immediately and pursuing your negotiations at the same time. That way, if you run out of time and have not been able to work out anything with your creditor, you do not risk having the stay automatically lifted without having the option of a court hearing. Should such a motion be requested, your attorney should respond immediately, assuming you want to fight the motion to lift the automatic stay.**

---

Usually, if certain assets are necessary for your reorganization, the court will let you keep them despite your creditors' objections. However, the court will probably require that you make *adequate protection* payments to your creditors.

The best way to deal with the possibility that your creditors will object to your use of collateral essential to your business is to negotiate agreements with them as soon as you file. Have your attorney talk with your creditors about how much money it will take for them to feel that their collateral is adequately protected. Then, you can file the appropriate documents with the court and seek court approval to make the payments while waiting for your plan to be approved. A hearing may be held.

As this chapter has already indicated, the use of cash collateral is a common source of debtor-creditor friction in Chapter 11 once a bankruptcy has been filed. Cash collateral often represents the first issue that you will do battle over.

## Administrative Expenses

Administrative costs in Chapter 11 can be substantial. They may include the fees of outside professionals, such as attorneys, accountants and appraisers, as well as other bankruptcy-related expenses incurred after filing. These costs must be paid from your bankruptcy estate before any of your debts can be paid. Therefore, in an effort to maximize the amount of money available to pay them, your creditors may contest your right to incur outside expenses as well as the amount of those expenses.

## Bringing in a Private Trustee

Prior to confirmation, if your creditors feel that you are not running your business in a responsible manner, a hearing will be held, and a private trustee may be appointed to take over your business management responsibilities. Involving a private trustee can be a very serious turn of events since the trustee appointed to run your business may not know anything about your industry.

## The Reorganization Plan Approval Process

You must file your reorganization plan within 120 days of filing your bankruptcy. For your plan to be approved, more than half of all claims in each impaired class of creditors and at least two-thirds of the total dollar value of all the claims in a class, must vote in favor of your reorganization plan. If you are incorporated, your plan must also be approved by a majority of your shareholders. To vote, your creditors will be sent ballots for voting, together with copies of your disclosure statement and your reorganization plan.

---

### Survival Tip #129

**Unimpaired creditors will not vote on your reorganization plan because they are assumed to approve it.**

---

The bankruptcy judge will base a decision to approve or disapprove your plan on the plan's adequacy, fairness and whether it complies with all provisions of the bankruptcy code. Typically, if all impaired classes approve your plan, the court will also approve it.

## Survival Tip #130

**Failure to file your plan before the 120-day deadline is up means that you risk the possibility that your creditors will prepare their own plans.**

If a class of creditors does not approve your reorganization plan, the court may still approve it against the creditors' wishes if the court believes that the plan is fair to that class. When this happens, it is called a cram-down.

## Survival Tip #131

**The specific circumstances under which a cram-down can be applied vary depending on whether it is directed toward secured or unsecured creditors or shareholders.**

Forcing your creditors to accept your reorganization plan can seriously complicate your bankruptcy, causing delays, added expense and greater involvement of the court in your bankruptcy. Although a cram-down should be considered an option of last resort, cramming down creditors may be the only way you can successfully reorganize.

## Survival Tip #132

**When possible, it is best to identify those creditors that you expect will not accept your reorganization plan, isolate them into a single class of creditors and try to get the court to enforce the cram-down provision against that class only.**

If the court fails to approve your plan, you'll have an opportunity to prepare a new one and to get it approved.

# Confirmation

Approval of your reorganization plan will signal the end of your bankruptcy and the end of the court's active involvement in your business's activities. At this time, you will receive a discharge.

---

### Survival Tip #133

**Even though your debts are discharged, you must pay your debts according to the terms of your reorganization plan.**

---

If your business is a partnership or a corporation, all debts but those delineated in the reorganization plan will be discharged.

Once your plan has been confirmed, you will be expected, as the debtor in possession, to run your business in accordance with the terms of your reorganization plan. You will be expected to make all debt payments in full and on time and to make decisions that are in the best interest of all your creditors.

---

### Survival Tip #134

**After your plan has been confirmed and your business has been operating under its terms, it will be difficult, if not impossible, to modify your reorganization plan if it is not working out or needs to be changed for some other reason. A Chapter 7 bankruptcy may be your only option.**

---

# Dismissal of a Chapter 11

It is possible at some point during the Chapter 11 process that the court will dismiss your bankruptcy, forcing you to find another way to address your financial problems. Dismissal can occur before or after your plan has been confirmed. The conditions under which dismissal can happen include:

- You are unable to prepare a reorganization plan by the deadline.

- You are unable to get a majority of your creditors to approve your plan by the deadline.
- You fail to pay the trustee all necessary fees.
- You fail to meet the terms of your reorganization plan after it is confirmed.

## Conclusion

As this book has stressed, Chapter 11 is not a good choice for most small businesses due to its expense, complexity and the amount of power creditors can wield. All too often, small business owners who file this type of bankruptcy find that they spend so much time dealing with the details of Chapter 11 that they are unable to do what it takes to turn their businesses around. Ultimately, many businesses in Chapter 11 convert to Chapter 7, closing their businesses down.

Small businesses that do not qualify for a Chapter 13 reorganization and want to use Chapter 11 to reorganize should seek the advice and assistance of an experienced Chapter 11 bankruptcy attorney as soon as possible. The earlier business owners seek professional assistance, the more likely their Chapter 11 bankruptcies will be a success.

Although much of the Chapter 11 process mirrors the Chapter 13 process, there are some important differences: A business's reorganization plan must be approved by both the court and its creditors. The business as the debtor in possession acts as its own trustee and will be expected to make debt payments directly to its creditors and to make business decisions that are in its creditors' best interests.

# Epilogue

# Looking toward the Future

### *Strategy for Success*

*Four years ago, a local bank invited me to speak at a seminar on starting a small business. A young man named Dan F. came up after the program to ask me a few questions. He had been struck by my advice to members of the audience that they "talk to a bankruptcy attorney before starting their businesses." That comment surprised and confused Dan, and he wanted to know more, especially since he was in the process of investing his savings in a drive-in grocery store.*

*Dan and I talked about several issues that arise when starting a business and the importance of keeping in mind that failure is always possible. Dan said that he had considered some but not all of the points I had raised.*

*After our talk, Dan hired me to consult with him about the start-up of his business. Dan had wisely concluded that if he knew why other small business owners failed, he could avoid making the same mistakes and would increase his chances for success.*

*Soon after, Dan began calling me regularly. We discussed such issues as where to locate his business and whether he should lease or buy a store location. We also talked about the appropriate legal form for his business. Since both Dan's suppliers and his bank required personal guarantees, I recommended that Dan begin operating as a sole proprietorship.*

*Dan and I also discussed how to protect his personal assets in the event that his business failed, as well as the management skills and knowledge that he needed to have in order to run a successful business. I was able to answer some of Dan's questions, and I referred him to the appropriate professionals to answer the others.*

*Gradually, Dan's calls tapered off. I now hear from him only occasionally—usually when he is about to make an important business decision and wants to discuss its possible ramifications.*

---

Dan's business has thrived, and he is a real "American success story." Much of Dan's success can be credited to his determination to take as few risks as possible when getting his business started as well as his dedication to learning everything he could about running a successful drive-in grocery store before opening his own. Dan actually managed someone else's store before buying his own to ensure that he enjoyed the work.

Luck is almost always an important ingredient for entrepreneurial success! Soon after Dan opened his store, a large housing development went in less than a mile from his location, providing him with a seemingly endless supply of customers.

Dan is a textbook example of the ideal entrepreneur. He did everything right, and everything worked in his favor. Dan made sure that he would enjoy and had the temperament to run his own business; he sought the advice of experts before beginning his business; he made certain that he chose the appropriate legal structure; he was able to obtain adequate financing; he took steps to protect his personal assets in the event of financial trouble; and he did everything else possible to reduce his risks.

Unfortunately, as this book has clearly pointed out, Dan's very systematic and deliberate approach to his business—and the success he achieved—are not typical of most small business owners. All too often, aspiring entrepreneurs go into business without doing much up-front planning, with poor management skills, no clear understanding of what it will take to be successful and limited knowledge of how to identify and deal with business problems.

If this description applies to you, it's likely that you've experienced some tough times as a small business owner. Weathering those tough times and emerging from them stronger and more prepared for the future is in large part a function of attitude. A positive attitude asks, "What have I learned from all of this, and how can I benefit from my business troubles?" Such an attitude is likely to provide you with the inner resources and resolve that you need to either create future business success for yourself or to find a rewarding job with a good employer if you decide that running your own business is not for you.

Don't lose sight of the fact that starting and running a small business and struggling to keep it alive have provided you with the experiences, skills and knowledge that no MBA program could ever offer! Along the way, you have also gained important insight into yourself, discovering talents and qualities that you may not have realized you had and gaining a better appreciation of your limitations as well. These experiences can help you create a positive future for yourself regardless of what you decide to do.

## Take Time for Reflection

It is beneficial to spend some time reflecting on the lessons you've learned and to commit your thoughts to paper so that you do not forget what you've learned from your financial struggles. To trigger your thinking, ask yourself the following questions:

- What are the key things I've learned about managing a business?
- What would I do differently, and what would I do the same?
- What do I like about being in business, and what don't I like?
- What did I learn about myself?

This exercise can help you put your difficulties in perspective and map out a future course of action. It can also help you avoid repeating past mistakes.

Although self-reflection can be very helpful, do not let it turn into self-recrimination. It is important not to dwell on the role your own management errors or lack of skills and knowledge may have played in creating your business's problems. It is important to be realistic about how you contributed to the problems to ensure that past mistakes are not repeated, but don't fall into the trap of labeling yourself a failure. Negative thinking will sap your energy, shake your confidence and inhibit your efforts to get on with your business, to start a new one or to reenter the job market. Keep in mind that if your business experienced serious difficulties, it is not the exception; it's the rule!

## A Wholesale Decision

*If a prize were given for facing the most adversity, Sylvia G. would certainly be in the running to win it. By the time she and her husband Henry had come to see me, there was little hope for their small neighborhood bar. They were deeply in debt, and their business was not making a profit. A liquidation bankruptcy was the obvious solution.*

*During the six months that the bankruptcy lasted, Sylvia's father died and Henry left her. Sylvia felt like she was walking in a cloud of disaster! Everything around her was going wrong.*

*I liked Sylvia and was concerned about her. She and I spent time talking about her plans for the future. Despite everything that she had been through, Sylvia was the kind of person who always had hope. She also had the ability to think constructively about solutions to her problems even when she had every right to feel overwhelmed by them. Therefore, while coping with the details and the emotions of her bankruptcy, divorce and her father's death, Sylvia never gave up on being in business.*

*Like many small neighborhood bar owners, Sylvia's business had always operated with too little cash. As a result, Sylvia was unable to maintain a sufficient inventory of beer for her bar. This meant that on weekends Sylvia usually had to buy beer at retail prices from local grocery stores so that she would have something to sell to her patrons. Consequently, Sylvia had not been making the profit that she needed to keep her business going.*

*As Sylvia thought about what to do next and mulled over the various things that had contributed to her business's demise, a new business opportunity came to mind. Since the inventory problems she experienced were shared by other small bar owners in her area, Sylvia decided to begin a wholesale beer company that would be open long hours seven days a week. Her business would sell beer to small bars at prices a little above wholesale.*

*Sylvia was able to raise enough money, and with the help of the major beer distributors in her area, she eventually opened her new business. Sylvia's store was an instant hit, and several years after opening, it continues to be a great success. Although Sylvia had gone through a lot, including a failed marriage, the death of a close family member and bankruptcy, she believed in herself, learned from her mistakes and was determined to have a successful small business.*

## Keys to Success

If you are currently in business or are ready to start a new one, don't allow the promise of your endeavor and the excitement of pursuing it to overshadow the advice and warnings in this book. Always bear in mind the keys to business success:

- Plan adequately up front.
- Seek the advice and guidance of outside professionals, including a reputable bankruptcy attorney.
- Hone your management skills.
- Know your limitations and how to compensate for them.
- Select the most appropriate legal structure for your business.
- Obtain adequate financing, but keep debt to a minimum.
- Regularly monitor your business's financial reports, and pay attention to the day-to-day details of running your business.
- Act quickly and decisively at the first sign of business trouble.
- Take advantage of no-cost/low-cost sources of assistance.
- Keep current with all tax obligations.
- Constantly monitor changes in the economy that may affect your business, suppliers or your customer base.
- Remain technologically competitive.
- Market effectively.
- Plan for growth.
- Understand the amount of hard work and sacrifice that is required to start and grow a profitable small business.

---

### Back on Track

*Like Johnny V., some people are determined not to give up on a business and will make serious sacrifices to make that business work. However, when I first met with Johnny to discuss his failing pawn shop, I had real doubts that he'd be able to save his business no matter what he did.*

*Looking at Johnny's cash flow statements, it was obvious that his business was cash poor. His pawn shop was unable to make many loans. During our meeting, we talked about whether Johnny should reorganize or close down his business. Johnny was not enthusiastic about either option. Instead, he was determined to save his business by turning it around.*

*We talked about the things that Johnny would have to do if his turnaround were to succeed. After our meeting, Johnny left my office ready to do what it would take to make his business profitable. With the help of a SCORE volunteer, Johnny carefully analyzed each of his expenses and eliminated every item that wasn't absolutely necessary. Johnny let his only employee go and began doing everything himself. And, he met with his creditors, suppliers and banker.*

*Although Johnny's initial actions improved his business's financial condition, his business still did not show a profit. Therefore, Johnny had to do more. In a dramatic demonstration of his commitment to keeping his business alive, Johnny gave up his apartment and began sleeping on a cot in his pawn shop storeroom and cooking on a hot plate. Johnny lived like this for months. Gradually the pawn shop's cash flow improved, and it began to show a small profit.*

*Today, Johnny's business is back on track. Johnny no longer lives in his pawn shop, and his business earns him a good living. Not every business can be turned around like Johnny's pawn shop. To accomplish what he did, Johnny took a risk and made extreme sacrifices that paid off.*

---

## Conclusion

Success as a small business owner can be one of life's most exciting and rewarding challenges. But, as this book has emphasized, success is often an uphill battle achieved only through good planning, hard work, attention to details and effective problem solving. If you experience business failure or serious financial problems, remember that they do not signal "the end of the world." In fact, as this epilogue has emphasized, financial problems are actually opportunities to develop new skills and knowledge and to discover your inner strengths.

An Arabic proverb states that we "learn little from success, but much from failure." Sylvia and Johnny, the subject of two anecdotes in this chapter, are certainly inspirational examples of the truth of this statement. Although the story of Dan's deliberate and analytic approach to his business is certainly impressive, the stories of Sylvia and Johnny are equally compelling. Whatever your future—small business owner or employee—these three entrepreneurs offer a convincing argument for what you can accomplish through hard work, sacrifice, ingenuity and commitment to a goal. They are excellent role models for us all.

# Appendix A

# Resources for Small Businesses

*T*he organizations and publications listed below can help small business owners do a better job of managing their business and dealing with financial problems.

## Associations and Organizations

*American Management Association*
135 W. 50th St.
New York, NY 10020
(212) 586-8100
Features *Growing Companies* Program, which sponsors classes in planning, management, finance and other topics targeted toward the small-sized to medium-sized company

*Center for Entrepreneurial Management*
180 Varick St., 17th Fl.
New York, NY 10014
(212) 633-0060
Offers books, video products and other business management resources for small business owners

*National Association for the Self-Employed*
PO Box 612067
DFW Airport, TX 75261
(800) 232-NASE
A small business advice hotline and other services

*National Association of Women Business Owners*
600 S. Federal St., Ste. 400
Chicago, IL 60605
(312) 922-0465
Networking group

*National Business Incubation Association*
1 President St.
Athens, OH 45701
(614) 593-4331
Business incubators providing a variety of assistance to promising start-up businesses

*National Small Business United*
1155 15th St., NW, Ste. 710
Washington, DC 20005
(202) 293-8830
Lobbies Capitol Hill to help small businesses fight bureaucracy and regulations; regional chapters sponsor business seminars

# Federal Government Resources

### Small Business Administration (SBA)

The SBA offers a wide variety of excellent publications related to all aspects of running a business. For information about SBA publications, write:

SBA Publications
PO Box 1000
Fort Worth, TX 76119
The SBA provides assistance, training and educational programs, as well as counseling, to small business owners through the following programs:

**Service Corps of Retired Executives (SCORE)** Volunteer retired executives offer one-on-one business management counseling and advice in communities across the country.

In addition, the SBA helps small businesses obtain financing through its loan guarantee programs and specialized loan programs. It also maintains an export assistance program and a federal government procurement assistance program. For information about these and other SBA programs in your community, call your local SBA office (listed in the phone directory under federal government) or (800) U-ASK-SBA (827-5722).

**Small Business Development Centers (SBDCs)** Located on college campuses, at state government offices and local Chambers of Commerce; provide assistance and counseling.

**Small Business Institutes (SBIs)** On college campuses across the country; graduate students and professors offer free management studies to small businesses.

## Government Publications

**Consumer Information Center (CIC)** This office offers a wide selection of publications dealing with consumer and business issues. To obtain a catalog, write:

Consumer Information Center
PO Box 100
Pueblo, CO 81002

**Government Printing Office (GPO)** This federal government office sells many publications related to business management. To obtain a list of available publications and their costs, write:

Government Printing Office
Superintendent of Documents
Washington, DC 29402-9328

Some cities also have GPO bookstores. To find out if there is one in your city, look in the *Yellow Pages* under bookstores.

# Other Publications

### Brochures

*Bank Financing for New and Growing Businesses*. Suttmiller & Associates, 11516 N. Port Washington Rd., Mequon, WI 53092.

*Dun & Bradstreet's Challenges of Managing a Small Business*, Free. Debbie Thornberry, Dunn & Bradstreet, (800) 367-7782.

### Magazines

*Entrepreneur*, PO Box 1987, Irvine, CA 92713-9787, (800) 421-2300.

*In Business*, J.G. Press, PO Box 323, Emmaeus, PA 18049.

*Inc.*, 38 Commercial Wharf, Boston, MA 02110, (617) 248-8000.

*Nation's Business*, PO Box 51602, Boulder, CO 80321-1062, (800) 638-6582. A Chamber of Commerce publication.

*Small Business Reports*, 135 W. 50th St., New York, NY 10020, (212) 903-8160.

*Success*, PO Box 3036, Harlan, IA 51593-2097, (800) 234-7324.

*Your Company*, 1120 Avenue of the Americas, New York, NY 10039, (212) 392-5739. Available to holders of the corporate American Expresscard.

### Books

*The Bankruptcy Kit: Understanding the Bankruptcy Process, Knowing Your Options, Making a Fresh Start*, John Ventura, Dearborn Financial Publishing.

*Borrowing for Your Business*, George M. Dawson, Upstart Publishing Company, Inc.

*Buying and Selling Business: A Step-By-Step Guide*, John Wiley & Sons, Inc.

*The Cash Flow Control Guide*, David A. Bangs, Jr., Upstart Publishing Company, Inc.

*Cash Flow Problem Solver*, Bryan Milling, Sourcebooks.

*The Complete Guide to "S" Corporations*, Ted Nicholas, Enterprise • Dearborn.

*The Complete Small Business Legal Guide*, Robert Friedman, Enterprise • Dearborn.

*Coopers & Lybrand Guide to Growing Your Own Business*, Available through Coopers & Lybrand offices.

*Financial Troubleshooting: An Action Plan for Money Management in the Small Business*, David A. Bangs, Jr. and the editors of *Common Sense*, Upstart Publishing Company, Inc.

*Finding Money for Your Small Business*, Max Fallek, Enterprise • Dearborn.

*Guerilla Marketing: Secrets for Making Big Profits from Your Small Business*, J. Conrad Levinson, Houghton Mifflin.

*How To Form Your Own Corporation Without a Lawyer for under $75*. Ted Nicholas, Enterprise • Dearborn.

*How To Get a Business Loan*, Joseph Mancuso, Random House.

*How To Really Start Your Own Business*, David E. Gumpert, Goldhirsch Group, Inc.

*Keeping the Books: Basic Recordkeeping and Accounting for the Small Business*, Linda Pinson and Jerry Jinnett, Upstart Publishing Company, Inc.

*Keys to Starting a Small Business*, Joel Siegel and Jae K. Shim, Barrons.

*The Legal Guide for Starting & Running a Small Business*, Fred Steingold, Nolo Press.

*Managing by the Numbers: Financial Essentials for the Growing Business*, David A. Bangs, Jr., Upstart Publishing Company, Inc.

*Marketing Sourcebook for Small Businesses*, Jeffrey P. Davidson, John Wiley Publishing.

*Marketing Without Advertising*, Michael Phillips and Salli Rasberry, Nolo Press.

*The Market Planning Guide*, David A. Bangs, Jr., Upstart Publishing Company, Inc.

*Money Sources for Small Businesses: How You Can Find Private, State, Federal, and Corporate Financing*, William Alarid, Puma Publishing.

*The New Small Business Survival Guide*, Bob Coleman, W.W. Norton & Company.

*On Your Own: A Woman's Guide to Building a Business*, Laurie Zuckerman, Upstart Publishing, Inc.

*Selling Your Business*, Paul S. Sperry and Beatrice H. Mitchell, Upstart Publishing Company, Inc.

*Small Business Sourcebook*, edited by Carol A. Schwartz, Gale Research.

*Small Business Survival Guide*, Robert Fleury, Sourcebooks, Inc.

*Stand Up to the IRS*, Fred Daily, Nolo Press.

*The Start-Up Guide: A One-Year Plan for Entrepreneurs*, David A. Bangs, Jr., Upstart Publishing Company, Inc.

*The Ted Nicholas Small Business Course*, Ted Nicholas, Enterprise • Dearborn.

*The Turnaround Survival Guide*, A. David Silver, Dearborn Financial Publishing, Inc.

# Appendix B

# IRS Forms

# How to prepare a Collection Information Statement

Complete all blocks, except shaded areas. Write "N/A" (Not Applicable) in those blocks that do not apply to you. *If you don't complete the form, we won't be able to help you determine the best method for you to pay the amount due.* The areas explained below are the ones we have found to be the most confusing to people completing the form.

## Section I

**Items 5e and 6e—Paydays**

Enter the frequency of your payday (weekly, biweekly, monthly, etc.) and on which day you are paid (Wednesday, Friday, etc.).

## Section III

**Item 13—Bank Accounts**

Enter all accounts even if there is currently no balance. *Do Not* enter bank loans.

**Item 14—Bank Charge Cards, Lines of Credit, etc.**

Enter only credit issued by a bank, credit union, or savings and loan (MasterCard, Visa, overdraft protection, etc.). List other charge accounts such as oil companies and department stores in Item 28.

**Item 16—Real Property Description and Ownership**

List all real estate that you own or are purchasing. Include the address, county, and type of buildings on the property. List the names of all owners and type of ownership (such as joint tenants, tenant in common, etc.).

**Item 17—Life Insurance**

Under the heading "type," indicate if it is whole life or term life.

## Section IV

**Items 24 thru 26—Vehicles, Real Property, and Other Assets**

**Current Market Value** - Indicate the amount you could sell the asset for today.

**Liabilities Balance Due** - Enter the current amount owed on the loan, mortgage, etc.

**Equity in Asset** - Subtract liability (current amount owed) from current market value.

**Date Pledged** - Enter the date the loan was originally taken out.

**Date of Final Payment** - Enter the date the loan will be fully paid. If you are behind in payments, enter "Behind."

List other assets you own such as campers, boats, jewelry, antiques, etc. in item 26.

**Item 28—Other Liabilities**

List all other liabilities, including charge accounts, bank loans and notes, personal loans, medical bills, etc.

## Section V

If only one spouse has a tax liability, but both have income, list the total household income and expenses.

\*U.S. Government Printing Office: 1991 — 282-014/43119

**Items 31 and 32—Wages/Salaries**

To determine net salary, deduct only mandatory items from your gross salary, such as social security and other withheld taxes, and company retirement. Do not deduct allotments you elect to take out of the check such as insurance payments, credit union deductions, car payments, etc. List these as expenses in **Section IV** and **Section V.**

**Item 34—Net Business Income**

If you are self employed, enter your monthly *Net* business income, that is, what you earn after you have paid your ordinary and necessary monthly business expenses.

## Necessary Living Expenses

Expenses must be reasonable for the size of your family, geographic location and unique circumstances.

**Item 42—Rent**

Enter your monthly rent payment. If you are a homeowner, write N/A.

**Item 44—Allowable Installment Payments**

Do not show any entry in this space. IRS use only.

**Item 45—Utilities**

Show the total utility expenses in the amount column. List the amount for each utility separately in the space beside that utility. If you need additional space, use the remarks area or a separate sheet of paper.

**Item 46—Transportation**

Enter the average monthly expense for gasoline, oil, parking, or public transportation.

**Item 47—Insurance**

Show the total insurance expenses in the amount column. List the amount for each insurance separately such as life, health, homeowners, and auto in the space beside it. If you need additional space, attach a separate sheet of paper.

**Item 48—Medical**

Show recurring medical expenses only. Do not include an occasional medical expense.

**Item 49—Estimated Tax Payments**

Enter the monthly average you pay on your estimated tax. Send a copy of your most recent canceled check or money order receipt as proof of payment.

**Items 52 and 53—Total and Net Difference**

Do not show an entry in these spaces. IRS use only.

## Certification

For joint income tax liabilities, both husband and wife should sign the statement.

Department of the Treasury
**Internal Revenue Service**
Catalog No. 61442W
Form 433-A Instructions (Rev. 6-91)

| Form **433-A** (Rev. October 1992) | Department of the Treasury — Internal Revenue Service  **Collection Information Statement for Individuals** |
|---|---|

NOTE: Complete all blocks, except shaded areas. Write "N/A" *(not applicable)* in those blocks that do not apply.

| 1. Taxpayer(s) name(s) and address | 2. Home phone number ( ) | 3. Marital status |
|---|---|---|
| County_____ | 4.a. Taxpayer's social security number | b. Spouse's social security number |

## Section I.       Employment Information

| 5. Taxpayer's employer or business *(name and address)* | a. How long employed | b. Business phone number ( ) | c. Occupation |
|---|---|---|---|
| | d. Number of exemptions claimed on Form W-4 | e. Paydays | f. *(Check appropriate box)* ☐ Wage earner    ☐ Partner   ☐ Sole proprietor |

| 6. Spouse's employer or business *(name and address)* | a. How long employed | b. Business phone number ( ) | c. Occupation |
|---|---|---|---|
| | d. Number of exemptions claimed on Form W-4 | e. Paydays | f. *(Check appropriate box)* ☐ Wage earner    ☐ Partner   ☐ Sole proprietor |

## Section II.       Personal Information

| 7. Name, address and telephone number of next of kin or other reference | 8. Other names or aliases | 9. Previous address(es) |
|---|---|---|

10. Age and relationship of dependents living in your household *(exclude yourself and spouse)*

| 11. Date of Birth ▶ | a. Taxpayer | b. Spouse | 12. Latest filed income tax return *(tax year)* | a. Number of exemptions claimed | b. Adjusted Gross Income |
|---|---|---|---|---|---|

## Section III.       General Financial Information

13. Bank accounts *(Include Savings & Loans, Credit Unions, IRA and Retirement Plans, Certificates of Deposit, etc.)*

| Name of Institution | Address | Type of Account | Account No. | Balance |
|---|---|---|---|---|
| | | | | |
| | | | | |
| | | | | |
| | | Total *(Enter in Item 21)* | | |

Form **433-A**  (Rev. 10-92)

## Section III - *continued*    General Financial Information

14. Bank charge cards, Credit Unions, Savings and Loans, Lines of credit

| Type of Account or Card | Name and Address of Financial Institution | Monthly Payment | Credit Limit | Amount Owed | Credit Available |
|---|---|---|---|---|---|
| | | | | | |
| | | | | | |
| | | | | | |
| | | | | | |
| **Totals** *(Enter in Item 27)* ▶ | | | | | |

15. Safe deposit boxes rented or accessed *(List all locations, box numbers, and contents.)*

| 16. Real Property *(Brief description and type of ownership)* | Physical Address |
|---|---|
| a. | County _____ |
| b. | County _____ |
| c. | County _____ |

| 17. Life Insurance *(Name of Company)* | Policy Number | Type | Face Amount | Available Loan Value |
|---|---|---|---|---|
| | | | | |
| | | | | |
| | | | | |
| **Total** *(Enter in Item 23)* ▶ | | | | |

18. Securities *(stocks, bonds, mutual funds, money market funds, government securities, etc.):*

| Kind | Quantity or Denomination | Current Value | Where Located | Owner of Record |
|---|---|---|---|---|
| | | | | |
| | | | | |
| | | | | |

19. Other information relating to your financial condition. If you check the yes box, please give dates and explain on page 4, Additional Information or Comments:

| | | | |
|---|---|---|---|
| a. Court proceedings | ☐ Yes ☐ No | b. Bankruptcies | ☐ Yes ☐ No |
| c. Repossessions | ☐ Yes ☐ No | d. Recent transfer of assets for less than full value | ☐ Yes ☐ No |
| e. Anticipated increase in income | ☐ Yes ☐ No | f. Participant or beneficiary to trust, estate, profit sharing, etc. | ☐ Yes ☐ No |

Form **433-A**   page 2   (Rev. 10-92)

## Section IV.　　　　　Asset and Liability Analysis

| Description | Current Market Value | Liabilities Balance Due | Equity in Asset | Amount of Monthly Payment | Name and Address of Lien/Note Holder/Obligee | Date Pledged | Date of Final Payment |
|---|---|---|---|---|---|---|---|
| 20. Cash | | | | | | | |
| 21. Bank accounts *(from Item 13)* | | | | | | | |
| 22. Securities *(from Item 18)* | | | | | | | |
| 23. Cash or loan value of Insur. | | | | | | | |
| 24. Vehicles *(Model, year, license, tag#)* | | | | | | | |
|   a. | | | | | | | |
|   b. | | | | | | | |
|   c. | | | | | | | |
| 25. Real property *(From Section III, item 16)*   a. | | | | | | | |
|   b. | | | | | | | |
|   c. | | | | | | | |
| 26. Other assets | | | | | | | |
|   a. | | | | | | | |
|   b. | | | | | | | |
|   c. | | | | | | | |
|   d. | | | | | | | |
|   e. | | | | | | | |
| 27. Bank revolving credit *(from Item 14)* | | | | | | | |
| 28. Other Liabilities *(Including judgments, notes, and other charge accounts)*   a. | | | | | | | |
|   b. | | | | | | | |
|   c. | | | | | | | |
|   d. | | | | | | | |
|   e. | | | | | | | |
|   f. | | | | | | | |
|   g. | | | | | | | |
| 29. Federal taxes owed | | | | | | | |
| 30. Totals | | $ | $ | | | | |

Internal Revenue Service Use Only Below This Line

## Financial Verification/Analysis

| Item | Date Information or Encumbrance Verified | Date Property Inspected | Estimated Forced Sale Equity |
|---|---|---|---|
| Personal Residence | | | |
| Other Real Property | | | |
| Vehicles | | | |
| Other Personal Property | | | |
| State Employment *(Husband and Wife)* | | | |
| Income Tax Return | | | |
| Wage Statements *(Husband and Wife)* | | | |
| Sources of Income/Credit *(D&B Report)* | | | |
| Expenses | | | |
| Other Assets/Liabilities | | | |

Form **433-A**　page 3　(Rev. 10-92)

## Section V.     Monthly Income and Expense Analysis

| Income | | | Necessary Living Expenses | |
|---|---|---|---|---|
| **Source** | **Gross** | **Net** | | |
| 31. Wages/Salaries *(Taxpayer)* | $ | $ | 42. Rent *(Do not show mortgage listed in item 25)* | $ |
| 32. Wages/Salaries *(Spouse)* | | | 43. Groceries (no. of people _____ ) | |
| 33. Interest - Dividends | | | 44. Allowable installment payments *(IRS use only)* | |
| 34. Net business Income *(from Form 433-B)* | | | 45. Utilities (Gas $_____ Water $_____ | |
| 35. Rental income | | | Electric $_____ Phone $_____ ) | |
| 36. Pension *(Taxpayer)* | | | 46. Transportation | |
| 37. Pension *(Spouse)* | | | 47. Insurance (Life $_____ Health $_____ | |
| 38. Child Support | | | Home $_____ Car $_____ ) | |
| 39. Alimony | | | 48. Medical *(Expenses not covered in item 47)* | |
| 40. Other | | | 49. Estimated tax payments | |
| | | | 50. Court ordered payments | |
| | | | 51. Other expenses *(specify)* | |
| | | | | |
| | | | | |
| | | | | |
| 41. Total Income | $ | $ | 52. Total Expenses *(IRS use only)* | $ |
| | | | 53. Net difference *(income less necessary living expenses)* *(IRS use only)* | $ |

| Certification | Under penalties of perjury, I declare that to the best of my knowledge and belief this statement of assets, liabilities, and other information is true, correct, and complete. |
|---|---|

| 54. Your signature | 55. Spouse's signature *(if joint return was filed)* | 56. Date |
|---|---|---|
| | | |

Additional information or comments:

---

**Internal Revenue Service Use Only Below This Line**

Explain any difference between Item 53 and the installment agreement payment amount:

| Name of originator and IDRS assignment number: | Date |
|---|---|
| | |

Form **433-B**
(Rev. April 1989)

Department of the Treasury — Internal Revenue Service

# Collection Information Statement for Businesses

*(If you need additional space, please attach a separate sheet)*

| 1. Name and address of business | 2. Business phone number | ( ) |
|---|---|---|

County_____

3. *(Check appropriate box)*

☐ Sole proprietor   ☐ Other *(specify)*
☐ Partnership   _____
☐ Corporation   _____

| 4. Name and title of person being interviewed | 5. Employer Identification Number | 6. Type of business |
|---|---|---|

**7. Information about owner, partners, officers, major shareholder, etc.**

| Name and Title | Effective Date | Home Address | Phone Number | Social Security Number | Total Shares or Interest |
|---|---|---|---|---|---|
| | | | | | |
| | | | | | |
| | | | | | |
| | | | | | |

## Section I.  General Financial Information

| 8. Latest filed income tax return ▶ | Form | Tax Year ended | Net income before taxes |
|---|---|---|---|

**9. Bank accounts** *(List all types of accounts including payroll and general, savings, certificates of deposit, etc.)*

| Name of Institution | Address | Type of Account | Account Number | Balance |
|---|---|---|---|---|
| | | | | |
| | | | | |
| | | | | |
| | | **Total** *(Enter in Item 17)* ▶ | | |

**10. Bank credit available** *(Lines of credit, etc.)*

| Name of Institution | Address | Credit Limit | Amount Owed | Credit Available | Monthly Payments |
|---|---|---|---|---|---|
| | | | | | |
| | | | | | |
| **Totals** *(Enter in Items 24 or 25 as appropriate)* ▶ | | | | | |

11. Location, box number, and contents of all safe deposit boxes rented or accessed

**Section I** — *continued*　　　　　**General Financial Information**

12. Real property

| Brief Description and Type of Ownership | Physical Address |
|---|---|
| a. | County _____ |
| b. | County _____ |
| c. | County _____ |
| d. | County _____ |

13. Life insurance policies owned with business as beneficiary

| Name Insured | Company | Policy Number | Type | Face Amount | Available Loan Value |
|---|---|---|---|---|---|
|  |  |  |  |  |  |
|  |  |  |  |  |  |
|  |  |  |  |  |  |
| | | **Total** (Enter in Item 19) | | ▶ | |

14. Additional information regarding financial condition (*Court proceedings, bankruptcies filed or anticipated, transfers of assets for less than full value, changes in market conditions, etc.; include information regarding company participation in trusts, estates, profit-sharing plans, etc.*)

15. Accounts/Notes receivable (*Include current contract jobs, loans to stockholders, officers, partners, etc.*)

| Name | Address | Amount Due | Date Due | Status |
|---|---|---|---|---|
|  |  | $ |  |  |
|  |  |  |  |  |
|  |  |  |  |  |
|  |  |  |  |  |
|  |  |  |  |  |
|  |  |  |  |  |
|  |  |  |  |  |
|  |  |  |  |  |
|  |  |  |  |  |
|  |  |  |  |  |
|  |  |  |  |  |
|  |  |  |  |  |
|  | **Total** (Enter in Item 18) ▶ | $ |  |  |

　　　　　Form **433-B** (Rev. 4-89)

## Section II.   Asset and Liability Analysis

| Description (a) | | Cur. Mkt. Value (b) | Liabilities Bal. Due (c) | Equity in Asset (d) | Amt. of Mo. Pymt. (e) | Name and Address of Lien/Note Holder/Obligee (f) | Date Pledged (g) | Date of Final Pymt. (h) |
|---|---|---|---|---|---|---|---|---|
| 16. Cash on hand | | | | | | | | |
| 17. Bank accounts | | | | | | | | |
| 18. Accounts/Notes receivable | | | | | | | | |
| 19. Life insurance loan value | | | | | | | | |
| 20. Real property (from Item 12) | a. | | | | | | | |
| | b. | | | | | | | |
| | c. | | | | | | | |
| | d. | | | | | | | |
| 21. Vehicles (Model, year, and license) | a. | | | | | | | |
| | b. | | | | | | | |
| | c. | | | | | | | |
| 22. Machinery and equipment (Specify) | a. | | | | | | | |
| | b. | | | | | | | |
| | c. | | | | | | | |
| 23. Merchandise inventory (Specify) | a. | | | | | | | |
| | b. | | | | | | | |
| 24. Other assets (Specify) | a. | | | | | | | |
| | b. | | | | | | | |
| 25. Other liabilities (Include notes and judgments) | a. | | | | | | | |
| | b. | | | | | | | |
| | c. | | | | | | | |
| | d. | | | | | | | |
| | e. | | | | | | | |
| | f. | | | | | | | |
| | g. | | | | | | | |
| | h. | | | | | | | |
| 26. Federal taxes owed | | | | | | | | |
| 27. Total | | | | | | | | |

Form **433-B** (Rev. 4-89)

## Section III.                                     Income and Expense Analysis

| The following information applies to income and expenses during the period _____to_____ | | Accounting method used | |
|---|---|---|---|
| **Income** | | **Expenses** | |
| 28. Gross receipts from sales, services, etc. | $ | 34. Materials purchased | $ |
| 29. Gross rental income | | 35. Net wages and salaries   Number of Employees _____ | |
| 30. Interest | | 36. Rent | |
| 31. Dividends | | 37. Allowable installment payments *(IRS use only)* | |
| 32. Other income *(Specify)* | | 38. Supplies | |
| | | 39. Utilities/Telephone | |
| | | 40. Gasoline/Oil | |
| | | 41. Repairs and maintenance | |
| | | 42. Insurance | |
| | | 43. Current taxes | |
| | | 44. Other *(Specify)* | |
| 33. Total ▶ | $ | 45. Total *(IRS use only)* ▶ | $ |
| | | 46. Net difference *(IRS use only)* ▶ | $ |

**Certification**    Under penalties of perjury, I declare that to the best of my knowledge and belief this statement of assets, liabilities, and other information is true, correct, and complete.

| 47. Signature | 48. Date |
|---|---|
| | |

### Internal Revenue Service Use Only Below This Line

#### Financial Verification/Analysis

| Item | Date Information or Encumbrance Verified | Date Property Inspected | Estimated Forced Sale Equity |
|---|---|---|---|
| Sources of Income/Credit    (D&B Report) | | | |
| Expenses | | | |
| Real Property | | | |
| Vehicles | | | |
| Machinery and Equipment | | | |
| Merchandise | | | |
| Accounts/Notes Receivable | | | |
| Corporate Information, if Applicable | | | |
| U.C.C. : Senior/Junior Lienholder | | | |
| Other Assets/Liabilities: | | | |

Explain difference between Item 46 (or P&L) and installment agreement amount:  (If Form 433-A is not used)

| Name of Originator and IDRS assignment number | Date |
|---|---|
| | |

| Form **911** (Rev. April 1991) | Department of the Treasury — Internal Revenue Service **Application for Taxpayer Assistance Order *(ATAO)* to Relieve Hardship** |
|---|---|

**Note:** Filing this application may result in extending the statutory period of limitations. *(See instructions.)*

**Section I.**                              **Taxpayer Information**

| 1. Name*(s)* as shown on tax return | 2. SSN/EIN | 3. Spouse's SSN |
|---|---|---|
| | 4. Tax form | 5. Tax period ended |

| 6. Current address *(Number and street, apt. no., rural route)* | 7. City, town, or post office, state, and ZIP code |
|---|---|

| 8. Person to contact | 9. Telephone number ( ) | 10. Best time to call |
|---|---|---|

11. Description of problem *(If more space is needed, attach additional sheets.)*

12. Description of significant hardship and relief requested *(If more space is needed, attach additional sheets.)*

| 13. Signature of taxpayer or Corporate Officer *(See instructions.)* | 14. Date | 15. Signature of spouse shown in block 1 | 16. Date |
|---|---|---|---|

**Section II.**                    **Representative Information *(If applicable)***

| 17. Name of authorized representative | 18. Firm name |
|---|---|
| 19. Street address or P.O. Box | 20. City, town or post office, state, and ZIP code |

| 21. Telephone number ( ) | 22. Best time to call | 23. Centralized Authorization File *(CAF)* number |
|---|---|---|

| 24. Signature | 25. Date |
|---|---|

**Section III.**          *(For Internal Revenue Service only)*

| 26. Name of initiating employee | 27. ☐ IRS identified  ☐ Taxpayer request | 28. Telephone | 29. Function | 30. Office | 31. Date |
|---|---|---|---|---|---|

Cat. No. 16965S

Form **911** (Rev. 4-91)

# Instructions

**Purpose of form.**—You should use Form 911, Application for Taxpayer Assistance Order *(ATAO)* to Relieve Hardship, to apply for a review by the Taxpayer Ombudsman, or his designee, of actions being taken by the Internal Revenue Service. Such application may be made in cases where you are undergoing or about to undergo a significant hardship because of the manner in which the Internal Revenue laws are being administered. This application can not be used to contest the merits of any tax liability. If you disagree with the amount of tax assessed, please see Publication 1, Your Rights As A Taxpayer. While we are reviewing your application, we will take no further enforcement action. We will contact you after our review to advise you of our decision. The Internal Revenue Code requires us to suspend applicable statutory periods of limitation until a decision is made on your request.

**Where to file.**—This application should be addressed to the Internal Revenue Service, Problem Resolution Office in the district where you live. Call the local Taxpayer Assistance number listed in your telephone directory or 1-800-829-1040 for the address of the Problem Resolution Office in your district. **If you live overseas,** mail your request to the Assistant Commissioner *(International),* Internal Revenue Service, Problem Resolution Office, P.O. Box 144817, L'Enfant Plaza Station, Washington, DC 20026-4817.

**CAUTION: Requests submitted to the incorrect office may result in delays.** We will acknowledge your request within one week of receiving it. If you do not hear from us within 10 days *(15 days for overseas addresses)* of submitting your application, please contact the Problem Resolution Office in the IRS office to which you sent your application.

## Section I. Taxpayer Information

1. **Name*(s)* as shown on tax return.** Enter your name as it appeared on the tax return for each period you are requesting assistance. If your name has changed since the return was submitted, you should still enter the name as it appeared on your return. If you filed a joint return, enter both names.

2. **SSN/EIN.** Enter your social security number *(SSN)* or the employer identification number *(EIN)* of the business, corporation, trust, etc., for the name you showed in block 1. If you are married, and the request is for assistance on a problem involving a joint return, enter the social security number in block 2 for the first name listed in block 1.

3. **Spouse's SSN.** If the problem involves a joint return, enter the social security number for the second name listed in block 1.

4. **Tax form.** Enter the tax form number of the tax form you filed for which you are requesting assistance. For example, if you are requesting assistance for a problem involving an individual income tax return, enter "1040." If your problem involves more than one tax form, include the information in block 11.

5. **Tax period ended.** If you are requesting assistance on an annually filed return, enter the calendar year or the ending date of the fiscal year for that return. If the problem concerns a return filed quarterly, enter the ending date of the quarter involved. If the problem involves more than one tax period, include the information in block 11.

6. and 7. **Self-explanatory.**

8. **Person to contact.** Enter the name of the person to contact about the problem. In the case of businesses, corporations, trusts, estates, etc., enter the name of a responsible official.

9. **Telephone number.** Enter the telephone number, including area code, of the person to contact.

10. **Self-explanatory.**

11. **Description of problem.** Describe the action*(s)* being taken *(or not being taken)* by the Internal Revenue Service that are causing you significant hardship. If you know it, include the name of the person, office, telephone number, and/or address of the last contact you had with IRS. Please include a copy of the most recent correspondence, if any, you have had with IRS regarding this problem.

12. **Description of significant hardship and relief requested.** Describe the significant hardship which is being caused by the Internal Revenue Service's action *(or lack of action)* as outlined in Section I, block 11. Please tell us what kind of relief you are requesting.

13 and 15. **Signature*(s)*.** In order to suspend applicable statutory periods of limitations, you must sign this form in Section I, block 13 and block 15, if applicable; or your authorized representative, acting in your behalf, must sign in Section II, block 24. If your name has changed from the name that appears in Section I, block 1, sign using your current legal name. If the request is for assistance on a problem involving a joint return, both you and the spouse shown in block 1 must sign this form in order for the statutory period of limitations to be suspended. If one of the taxpayers is no longer living, the taxpayer's spouse or personal representative must sign the form and write "deceased" after the deceased taxpayer's name. If the taxpayer is your dependent child who can not sign this application because of age or other reasons, you may sign your child's name in the space provided followed by the words "By *(your signature),* parent *(or guardian)* for minor child." If the application is being made for other than an individual taxpayer, a person having authority to sign the return should sign the application. Enter the date the application is signed.

## Section II. Representative Information

If you are the taxpayer and you wish to have a representative act in your behalf, your representative must have a power of attorney of tax information authorization on file for the tax form*(s)* and period*(s)* involved. Complete Section II, blocks 17 through 23. *(See Form 2848, Power of Attorney and Declaration of Representative and Instructions for more information.)*

If you are an authorized representative and are submitting this request on behalf of the taxpayer identified in Section I, complete blocks 17 through 23. Sign and date this request in block 24 and block 25 and attach a copy of Form 2848, or the power of attorney.

23. **Centralized Authorization File *(CAF)* number.** Enter the representative's CAF number. The CAF number is the unique number that Internal Revenue Service assigns to a representative after a valid Form 2848 is filed with an IRS office.

---

## *(For IRS Use only)*

| ATAO code . | Date of determination | Statute suspended |
|---|---|---|
| | | ☐ No ☐ Yes: _____ days |
| How received | PRO signature | |

| Form **656**<br>(Rev. February 1992) | Department of the Treasury — Internal Revenue Service<br># Offer in Compromise | ▶**File in Triplicate**<br>▶**See Instructions**<br>Page 4 |
|---|---|---|

| Name and Address of Taxpayers | For Official Use Only | |
|---|---|---|
| | Offer is *(Check applicable box)*<br>☐ Cash *(Paid in full)*<br>☐ Deferred payment | Serial Number<br><br>*(Cashier's stamp)* |

| Social Security Number | Employer Identification Number | |
|---|---|---|

| To: **Commissioner of Internal Revenue Service** | Amount Paid<br>$ |
|---|---|

(1)  This offer is being submitted by taxpayer-proponents to compromise a tax liability, plus statutory additions resulting from the failure to pay an Internal Revenue liability described as follows: _____

*(Describe the specific tax liability, see instructions)*

_____

_____

_____

(2)  The total sum of the offer is $ _____ . If payment in full is not submitted with this offer, describe below when the payment will be made:

_____

_____

As required by section 6621 of the Internal Revenue Code, interest shall accrue on payments made from the date the offer is accepted and until the amount offered is paid in full. The interest will be compounded daily as required by Section 6622 of the Internal Revenue Code.

(3)  All payments made with this offer are submitted voluntarily. The taxpayer-proponents request that the offer be accepted to compromise the tax liability described in paragraph (1). If the offer is rejected or withdrawn, the amount deposited will be refunded unless the taxpayer-proponents authorize in writing that the payment be applied to the liability. If an authorization is made, the date of payment will be considered the date the offer is rejected or withdrawn.

(4)  In making this offer and as part of the consideration for the offer, the taxpayer-proponents agree: (a) to comply with all the provisions of the Internal Revenue Code relating to the filing of returns and the paying of taxes for a period of five (5) years following the acceptance of the offer; (b) that the United States shall retain all payments and credits made and applied to the tax liabilities being compromised, until the terms of the offer are satisfied; (c) that the United States shall be entitled to keep all amounts, including interest and penalties due to the taxpayer-proponents under the Internal Revenue laws because of any overpayment of any tax or other liability, for periods ending before the calendar year or extending through the calendar year in which the offer is accepted, and (d) to immediately return to the Internal Revenue Service any overpayment amount identified in (c) above, following the acceptance of the offer.

(5)  The total amount that can be collected under the terms and conditions of this offer cannot exceed the amount of the tax liabilities being compromised plus statutory additions.

(6)  It is also agreed that payments made under the terms of the offer shall be applied first to tax and penalty, in that order, due for the earliest tax period covered by this offer, then to tax and penalty for each succeeding tax period covered by this offer. No amount shall be applied to payment of interest until the tax and penalty liabilities for all tax periods covered by this offer have been paid.

(7)  It is agreed that upon notice to the taxpayer-proponents that the offer has been accepted, the taxpayer-proponents shall have no right to contest in court or otherwise the amount of the liability to be compromised. In addition, if there is a default on any payment or any other condition required under the terms of the offer, the Commissioner of the Internal Revenue Service or delegated official, may (a) proceed immediately by suit to collect the entire unpaid balance of the offer; (b) proceed immediately by suit to collect as liquidated damages an amount equal to the liability sought to be compromised, minus any payments already received under the terms of the offer with interest on the unpaid balance accruing and applied as specified in paragraph (2), from the date of default; or (c) disregard the amount of the offer and apply all amounts previously paid under the offer against the amount of the liability compromised and, without further notice of any kind, assess and collect by levy or suit the balance of the liability. The right to appeal to the United States Tax Court and the statutory restrictions against assessment and collection are waived upon acceptance of this offer as stated in paragraph (8).

(8)  The taxpayer-proponents agree to the waiver and suspension of any statutory periods of limitations for assessment and collection of the tax liability described in paragraph (1) while the offer is pending, during the time any amount offered remains unpaid and for one (1) year after the satisfaction of the terms of the offer. The offer shall be deemed pending from the date an authorized official of the Internal Revenue Service accepts taxpayer-proponents' waiver of the statutory periods of limitation and shall remain pending until an authorized official of the Internal Revenue Service formally, in writing, accepts, rejects or withdraws the offer. If there is an appeal with respect to this offer, the offer shall be deemed pending until the date the Appeals office formally accepts or rejects this offer in writing. If within thirty (30) days of being notified of a right to protest a determination with regard to this offer, no protest is filed, the taxpayer-proponents agree to waive the right to a hearing before the Appeals office for this offer in compromise.

(9)  The following facts and reasons are submitted as grounds for acceptance of this offer: _____

_____

*(If space is insufficient, please attach a supporting statement)*

(10)  It is understood that this offer will be considered and acted upon in due course and that it does not relieve the taxpayers from the liability sought to be compromised unless and until the offer is accepted in writing by the Commissioner or a delegated official, and there has been full compliance with the terms of the offer.

| I accept the waiver of statutory period of limitations for the Internal Revenue Service. | Under penalties of perjury, I declare that I have examined this offer, including accompanying schedules and statements, and to the best of my knowledge and belief, it is true, correct and complete. | |
|---|---|---|
| Signature of authorized Internal Revenue Service Official | Signature of Taxpayer-proponent | Date |
| Title                    Date | Signature of Taxpayer-proponent | Date |

Part 1 IRS Copy                                                          Form **656** (Rev. 2-92)

Page 2

## For Office Use Only

| Liability Incurred By *(List taxpayers included under same account no.)* | Kind of Liability *(Complete description)* | |
|---|---|---|
| **Date Notice of Lien Filed** | **Place Notice of Lien Filed** | **Was Bond Filed?** *(If yes, attach copy)* ☐ Yes ☐ No |
| **Were Assets Pledged as Security?** *(If yes, attach complete information)* | **Periods Involved and Dates Returns Filed for Offers Involving Delinquency Penalties Only** | **Were Tax Collection Waivers Filed?** *(If yes, attach copies)* ☐ Yes ☐ No |

## Attach Transcript of Accounts

Form **656** (Rev. 2-92)

# Instructions

## Background

Section 7122 of the Internal Revenue Code allows delegated Service officials to compromise a tax liability prior to its being referred to the Department of Justice. The term "tax liability" includes all penalty, interest, additional amount or addition to tax.

## Reason for Compromise

The service is allowed to compromise a liability for only one (1) or both of the following two (2) reasons:

(1)   doubt as to whether the taxpayer owes the liability
(2)   doubt that the liability can be collected in full

The Service cannot legally accept a compromise where the liability has already been decided by a court and/or there is no doubt that the liability can be collected.

If If you are submitting an offer based on doubt that the liability is owed, you must include with Form 656 a written statement which describes in detail why you believe that you do not owe the liability. If you are making the offer based on doubt as to our ability to collect your liability, you must include with Form 656 a statement which describes in detail why you believe the Service cannot collect more than offered from your assets and your present and future income, taking into consideration that the Service generally has ten (10) years to collect your liability. If you have assets or income which may be available to you but not to the Service for collection action, you must also explain why we should not expect some portion of these assets or income to be paid to the Service if we are to compromise your liability for less than you owe.

## Service Policy

The Service will accept an offer in compromise when it is unlikely that the tax liability can be collected in full and the amount offered reasonably reflects collection potential. An offer in compromise is a legitimate alternative to declaring a case as currently not collectible or to a protracted installment agreement. The goal is to achieve collection of what is potentially collectible at the earliest possible time and at the least cost to the Government.

In cases where an offer in compromise appears to be a viable solution to a tax delinquency, the Service employee assigned the case will discuss the compromise alternative with the taxpayer and, when necessary, assist in preparing the required forms. The taxpayer will be responsible for initiating the first specific proposal for compromise.

The success of the compromise program will be assured only if taxpayers make adequate compromise proposal consistent with their ability to pay and the Service makes prompt and reasonable decisions. Taxpayers are expected to provide reasonable documentation to verify their ability to pay. The ultimate goal is a compromise which is in the best interest of both the taxpayer and the Service. Acceptance of an adequate offer will also result in creating for the taxpayer an expectation of and a fresh start towards compliance with all future filing and payment requirements.

## Practical Consideration

The Service's policy is that the ultimate goal is a settlement which is both in the best interests of the Government and the taxpayer. It is your responsibility to show us why it would be in the Government's best interest to accept your proposal. When we consider your offer we must ask ourselves the following questions:

(1)   Could we collect more from the taxpayer than is offered? If the answer is "yes", you will either have to submit a larger offer or we must reject your offer.

(2)   Would we be better off waiting until some date in the future because all the evidence would indicate that collection in the future would result in more money than is offered? If the answer is "yes", you will either have to submit a larger offer amount or we must reject your offer.

(3)   Would the taxpaying public believe that the acceptance of your offer was a correct action. If the answer is "no", you either have to submit a larger offer or we would have to reject your offer.

The fact that you have no assets or income at this time from which the Service could collect the liability does not mean that the Service should simply accept anything that is offered because it represents all we can collect now. The Service does not operate on the theory that "something is better than nothing". For example it would not generally be in the Service's best interests to accept $25 on a $1,000 dollars liability or $1,000 on a $100,000 liability. It would generally be better for the Service to reject such nominal amount and wait to see what collection potential would arise during the remaining period of our ten-year collection period.

As we state in our policy, your offer will only be successful if, you submit a legitimate proposal that is in the Government's best interests.

## Additional Consideration

Generally the Service believes that you benefit if we accept your offer because you can conduct your financial life without the burden of a tax liability. Therefore, we may require further consideration for acceptance of your offer through the use of the following:

(1)   A written agreement that will require you to pay a percentage of future earnings.

(2)   A written agreement to relinquish certain present or potential tax benefits.

## Tax Compliance

Generally the Service will not accept an offer unless it is clear that the taxpayer will comply with all current filing requirements. You will note that the terms of the offer require future compliance for a period of five (5) years. Additionally, we will not accept your offer if you are not complying with all your current filing and paying requirements.

## Withholding Collection

Submission of an offer does not automatically suspend collection action on a liability. If there is any indication that the filing of the offer is solely for the purpose of delaying the collection of the tax or that delay would negatively impact our ability to collect the tax, we will continue collection efforts. If you have reached an agreement with the Service to make installment payments, those payments should continue.

## Specific Instructions

(1)   Form 656, Offer in Compromise, must be used to submit an offer. The form must be prepared in triplicate and filed in the district office of the Internal Revenue Service in your area. if you have been working with a specific service employee on your case, file the offer with that employee.

(2)   Form 433-A, Collection Information Statement for individuals and/or Form 433-B Collection Information Statement for Business, must accompany Form 656, if the offer is being submitted on the basis of doubt as to collectibility. In order for the offer to be considered, all blocks on forms 433-A and 433-B must be completed. In those blocks that do affect you indicate by writing "N/A" (not applicable). When you submit Form 433-A and/or 433-B documentation should be submitted to verify values of assets, encumbrances and income and expense information listed on the collection information statement.

(3)   Your full name, address and taxpayer identification number must be entered at the top of Form 656. If this is a joint liability (husband and wife) and both wish to make an offer, both names must be shown. If you are singly liable for a liability (e.g. employment taxes) and at the same time jointly liable for another liability (e.g. income taxes) and only one person is submitting an offer, only one offer must be submitted. If you are singly liable for one liability and jointly liable for another and both joint parties are submitting an offer, two (2) Forms 656 must be submitted, one (1) for the separate liability and one (1) for the joint liability.

(4)   You must list all unpaid liabilities to be compromised in item (1) on Form 656. The type of tax and the period of the liability must be specifically identified. Examples of the most common liabilities and the proper identification you should use are as follows:

| Liability | proper description |
| --- | --- |
| 1040 | Income tax for the year(s) 19XX... |
| 941 | Withholding and Federal Insurance Contribution Act taxes for the period(s) ended 09/30/XX, 12/31/XX... |
| 940 | Federal Unemployment Tax Act taxes for the year(s) 19XX... |
| 100 percent penalty | 100% penalty assessment incurred as a responsible person of Y Corporation for failure to pay withholding and Federal Insurance Contributions Act taxes for the periods ended 09/30/XX, 12/31/XX... |
| Failure to file penalty | Penalty for failure to file income tax return(s) for the tax year(s) 19XX... (Note: This is necessary only if your offer is submitted to compromise the penalty because of doubt as to liability) |

(5)   The total amount you are offering to compromise the liability must be entered in item (2). The amount must not include any amount which has already been paid or collected on the liability. Generally the starting place for the amount you offer should be the amount shown in item 27 column (d) in Form 433-B or line 37 titled "Equity in Assets" on form 433-A.

If any amount is to be paid on notice of acceptance of the offer or at any later date, you must include in item (2) as follows:

(a)   The amount, if any, deposited at the time of filing this offer.

(b)   Any amount deposited on a prior offer which are to be applied on this offer. (This does not include any amount you previously authorized the Service to apply directly to the tax liability)

(c)   The amount of any subsequent payment and the date on which each payment is to be made.

Example: $30,000 − $5,000 deposited with the offer and $25,000 to be paid within ten (10) days from the date of acceptance.

Example: $103,000 − $13,000 deposited with the offer and $10,000 to be paid within ten (10) days from the date of acceptance and $10,000 paid on the 15th of each month following the month in which the offer is accepted.

The offer should be liquidated in the shortest time possible. Under no circumstances should the payment extend beyond five (5) years from the date of acceptance to the date of full payment. Interest is due at the prevailing Internal Revenue Code rate from the date of acceptance to the date of full payment.

(6)   You must state in detail in item (9) why the Service should accept your offer. Attach additional pages as necessary.

(7)   You must sign and date the offer in the lower right hand corner of Form 656. If you and your spouse are submitting the offer on a joint liability both must sign. If the offer is to be signed by a person other than the taxpayer, a valid power of attorney must be submitted with the offer.

## What You Are Agreeing To

Please read Form 656 carefully so that you understand what you are agreeing to. Among other things you are agreeing to

1.   The suspension of any statutory period for assessment and collection of the tax liability while the offer is pending, during the time any amount offered remains unpaid and for one (1) year thereafter.
2.   Not to contest in court or otherwise appeal the amount of the liability if your offer is accepted.
3.   The giving up of overpayments (refunds) for all tax periods prior to and including the year the offer is accepted.
4.   The possible reinstatement of your entire tax liability, if you do not comply with all the terms of the offer, including the requirement for future compliance.

## Public Disclosure

You should be aware that the law requires that all accepted offers in compromise be available for review by the general public. Therefore it is possible that details of your personal financial affairs may become publicly known.

# Index